REVOLUTIONARY
REVELATION
BREAKING BARRIERS

A STUDY OF THE MOST IMPORTANT PRAYER
IN THE NEW TESTAMENT FOR BELIEVERS

Revolutionary Revelation
ISBN 978-1889981-512
Copyright © 2014 by Mark Hankins

Published by Mark Hankins Ministries
P.O. Box 12863
Alexandria, LA 71315
www.markhankins.org
318.767.2001

REVOLUTIONARY REVELATION

MARK HANKINS

Table of Contents

SECTION THREE: REVOLUTIONARY REVELATION BRINGS REVOLUTIONARY RESULTS

SECTION FOUR: REVOLUTIONARY RELATIONSHIPS

SECTION ONE:
REVELATION KNOWLEDGE

That the God of our Lord Jesus Christ, the Father of glory, may give unto you the spirit of wisdom and revelation in the knowledge of him: The eyes of your understanding being enlightened; that ye may know what is the hope of his calling, and what the riches of the glory of his inheritance in the saints, And what is the exceeding greatness of his power to us-ward who believe, according to the working of his mighty power, Which he wrought in Christ, when he raised him from the dead, and set him at his own right hand in the heavenly places, Far above all principality, and power, and might, and dominion, and every name that is named, not only in this world, but also in that which is to come: And hath put all things under his feet, and gave him to be the head over all things to the church, Which is his body, the fulness of him that filleth all in all.

Ephesians 1:17-23 (KJV)

1

The Secrets of God

The Gospel of Jesus Christ is not a human discovery, it is a revelation from God. The fact that God is as Jesus showed him to be is not something which a man could have discovered by intellectual processes. Man does not discover God. God reveals Himself. [1]

William Barclay

HIDE AND SEEK

There are things that are hidden for us in Christ. We sometimes think so much is hidden from us, yet

God has chosen "revelation" as His way. God seems to play hide and seek with us. The good news is when we seek Him, we will find Him when we search for Him with all our heart. God actually enjoys revealing Himself; He chooses to reveal Himself. Today we are at the threshold of an increase in the revelation of God that will launch a revolution that will change this generation.

> *In whom are hid all the treasures of wisdom*
> *and knowledge.*
> *Colossians 2:3*

A PROFOUND SECRET

REVOLUTION: to effect radical change; any fundamental complete change; the replacement of a government or political system. [2]

The Apostle Paul's revelation of Jesus Christ caused not only radical change in his life, but the lives of millions of people over the past 2000 years. Paul's revelation of the Gospel of Christ has unlocked the greatest of all mysteries. What God has revealed in

Christ has uncovered the eternal purpose for every man. God's love, God's power, God's goodness, God's righteousness, God's wisdom—all are revealed in the Gospel of Christ!

> *Therefore if any man be in Christ, he is a new creature, old things are passed away, behold all things are become new.*
> *2 Corinthians 5:17*

2 Corinthians 5:17 describes a radical change! A.J. Gordon said it this way, "These two words 'In Christ' give us profound insight into the Divine method of salvation. These two words open to us mysteries and secrets that were hidden for ages and generations." [3]

THE WHOLE ELEPHANT

I like to think of the story of the four blind men who were each holding on to a different part of an elephant. One held the tail and said an elephant was like a rope. One held the leg and said an elephant was like a tree. One held the trunk and said an elephant was like a snake. One felt the side of the elephant and said he was like a wall. Each man's revelation was limited to the part of the elephant he experienced.

Many of us are like that today with our relationship with God. God wants to open our eyes to see the whole elephant. There is more that God has for us. Revelation opens God's goodness and power to us and through us!

> *The important thing is not to stop questioning.*
> *Curiosity has its own reason for existing.*
> *One cannot help but be in awe when one*
> *contemplates the mysteries of eternity, of life, of*
> *the marvelous structure of reality. It is enough*
> *if one tries merely to comprehend a little of this*
> *mystery everyday.* [4]
> *Albert Einstein*

THE CHURCH ON DISPLAY—
THE WISDOM OF GOD

MYSTERY: a profound secret kept cautiously concealed, hidden for generations, something that excites curiosity and wonder. [5]

> *And to make all men see what is the fellowship*
> *of the mystery, which from the beginning of*
> *the world hath been hid in God, who created*
> *all things by Jesus Christ: To the intent that*
> *now unto the principalities and powers in*
> *heavenly places might be known by the church*
> *the manifold wisdom of God, according to the*
> *eternal purpose which he purposed in Christ*
> *Jesus our Lord.*
> *Ephesians 3:9-11*

Paul's prayer in Ephesians 1:17-23 is for the church to advance and influence every generation through the power of revelation. The mystery of our redemption is **NOW** revealed in Christ. Today, God wants the church to enjoy and display the light and revelation of Jesus Christ to all men as well as to the unseen powers in heavenly places. The church is displaying the many-sided wisdom of God to men, angels, and devils. The church is experiencing a breakthrough in revelation that is bringing a revolution to this generation. We contend for exponential increase in revelation. We contend for the glory of God in the church today.

[1] *William Barclay, New Testament Words*

[2] *www.merriam-webster.com, revolution*

[3] *A.J. Gordon, In Christ*

[4] *Reagan, Michael, The Hand of God.*

[5] *www.merriam-webster.com, mystery*

The fact that God is as Jesus showed Him to be is not something which a man could have discovered by intellectual processes. Man does not discover God. God reveals Himself to man.

William Barclay

2

This Changes Everything

When Jesus was raised from the dead, He DID NOT say, "I hope that helped you just a little bit." Jesus did not die and go through the suffering of the cross and being raised from the dead just to help us a little bit. He brings radical change! When Jesus was raised from the dead, He said, "All power in heaven and earth has been given to me." In Christ, old things have passed away and now everything is new. THIS CHANGES EVERYTHING!

I remember a time when I became very interested in Albert Einstein and his theory of relativity. I went to the store and bought several books, brought them home and started to read. The problem was, I realized this was way over my head and I actually needed the book, "Albert Einstein For Dummies." Then I happened across a televised documentary on how Einstein's breakthrough discoveries changed everything for physics.

Einstein's famous theory, $E=MC^2$, was a revolutionary revelation that forever changed the way scientists thought about how space and time relate to matter and energy. He apologized to Isaac Newton because they ended up having to re-write all of his physics books. This breakthrough completely changed the way we view the world by opening quantum physics and unlocking the atom and nuclear fission. He said, "This changes everything!" The Apostle Paul's revelation of who the believer is in Christ is much greater than Einstein's discovery. What God did in Christ has truly changed everything. The blood of Jesus has mightily prevailed in three separate places. It prevailed in Heaven, in hell, and in your heart. Let's take a look at His plan of redemption.

THE BLOOD FOREVER
CHANGED HEAVEN

*Therefore if any man be in Christ, he is a new
creature: old things are passed away; behold, all
things are become new.*

2 Corinthians 5:17

*The old state of things has passed away; a new
state of things has come into existence.*

Weymouth

When Jesus died on the cross, He became sin for us
and His death was the death of the sinful old creation.
Jesus' blood was the redeeming price paid to buy back
humanity from the power of Satan. It broke the curse
of sin and all its effects. Jesus Christ shed His blood,
defeated sin, was justified in the spirit and then raised
from the dead. As our Forerunner, He ascended and
took His blood into Heaven and placed it there in the
holy of holies. Hebrews 9:12 says, ***"Neither by the
blood of goats and calves, but by his own blood
he entered in once into the holy place, having
obtained eternal redemption for us."***

Jesus' blood opened Heaven for us. ***"Having therefore, brethren, boldness to enter into the holiest by the blood of Jesus,"*** Hebrews 10:19. Now the blood is on the altar before the Father, forever speaking of mercy and grace. His blood changed everything in Heaven!

THE BLOOD TRIUMPHS OVER HELL

And they overcame him by the blood of the Lamb, and by the word of their testimony; and they loved not their lives unto the death.
Revelation 12:11

And having spoiled principalities and powers, he made a shew of them openly, triumphing over them in it.
Colossians 2:15

I like Andrae Crouch's song referring to the blood of Jesus that says, "It reaches to the highest mountain and flows to the lowest valley."[1] Jesus triumphed over the devil in the confines of humanity as a God-Man. He defeated Satan for every man. Jesus triumphed over Satan himself with His own blood so that we can overcome as a new creation. Jesus' blood overcomes all the power of Satan and hell.

THE BLOOD CHANGES
YOUR HEART

And having an high priest over the house of God; Let us draw near with a true heart in full assurance of faith, having our hearts sprinkled from an evil conscience, and our bodies washed with pure water.
Hebrews 10:21, 22

This is the new covenant I will make with my people on that day, says the Lord: I will put my laws in their hearts, and I will write them on their minds.
Hebrews 10:16 (NLT)

Christ has brought you into the very presence of God and you are standing there before Him

> *with nothing left against you - nothing that He*
> *could even chide you for.*
> *Colossians 1:22 (TLB)*

Your heart has become the dwelling place for God, the meeting place between a righteous child and a Holy Father God. This changes everything in your heart.

ACCESS GRANTED

We were speaking in a church recently where all the staff wore a card on a string around their necks which had the word "Access" written on them. This key card gave them access to different areas and through various doors in the church. I noticed the pastor's card was different. It said, "UNLIMITED ACCESS." He could go freely into any area in the building others couldn't.

In Christ, by faith in his blood, believers access the most holy place in prayer. One cannot be in God's presence for a moment without being changed! Burdens are lifted, power is increased, revelation granted and the love, joy, faith, and fire of God are experienced. Paul, who knew the formality and deadness of religion and the old law of Moses, wrote about something that happens when any person in Christ accesses the throne room. He said in Ephesians 3:12, ***"In whom we have boldness and access...."***

> *All of us! Nothing between us and God, our faces shining with the brightness of his face. And so we are transfigured much like the Messiah, our lives gradually becoming brighter and more beautiful as God enters our lives and we become like him.*
> *2 Corinthians 3:18 (MSG)*

> *And the Lord — who is the Spirit —makes us more and more like him as we are changed into his glorious image.*
> *NLT*

> *And all of us ... are constantly being transfigured into His very own image in ever increasing splendor and from one degree of glory to another; [for this comes] from the Lord [Who is] the Spirit.*
> *AMP*

Because of the blood of Jesus, any person in Christ has been granted full access to the very presence of God. Let us take advantage of all that has been done to open Heaven, overcome hell and open our hearts to the glory of God. May you be granted, by the Spirit's power, a revolutionary revelation. ***This Changes Everything!***

[1] *Reagan, Michael, The Hand of God.*
[2] *www.allthelyrics.com*

I want to know how God created this world. I am not interested in this or that phenomenon, in the spectrum of this or that element. I want to know His thoughts; the rest are details.

Albert Einstein

That the God of our Lord Jesus Christ, the all-glorious Father,

will give you spiritual wisdom and the insight to know more of

him: that you may receive that inner illumination of the spirit

which will make you realize how great is the hope to which he is

calling you—the magnificence and splendour of the inheritance

promised to Christians—and how tremendous is the power

available to us who believe in God. That power is the same

divine energy which was demonstrated in Christ when he raised

him from the dead and gave him the place of supreme honour in

Heaven—a place that is infinitely superior to any conceivable

command, authority, power or control, and which carries with

it a name far beyond any name that could ever be used in this

world or the world to come. God has placed everything under

the power of Christ and has set him up as supreme head of

everything for the Church. For the Church is his body, and in

that body lives fully the One who fills the whole wide universe.

Ephesians 1:17-23 (Phillips)

3

Revolutionary Breakthrough

On October 14, 1947, Captain Charles E. "Chuck" Yeager became the first person to fly faster than the speed of sound. At 10:30 a.m. on that fall morning, Chuck piloted the X-1 to a speed of Mach 1.06 (700 mph) at 43,000 feet above the high desert of California. The sound barrier that many feared was broken.

Finding a man willing to risk the unknown of supersonic flight proved to be difficult; no man had ever been there. Some pilots called supersonic flight the "monster" while others called it the "ughknown." Many thought that no pilot or plane could withstand the stress of flying at such a speed. Others speculated that as soon as the sound barrier was broken, the airplane would disintegrate.

"A POKE THROUGH JELLO"

A pioneer and an American hero, Chuck Yeager, determined he would be the first to break the sound barrier. With this historic flight, Yeager ushered in the beginning of America's launch into outer space and NASA's modern space shuttle.

Breaking the sound barrier also broke the fear of the unknown. Yeager later described his supersonic flight as "a poke through jello," "sipping lemonade on the front porch," and "a perfectly paved speedway."[1] The real barrier was not in the sky; it was in man's lack of knowledge regarding supersonic flight.[2]

THE SPIRIT OF WISDOM

Christians often face challenges and barriers doing the will of God. Even the most difficult barriers can be broken, and believers can go to places in God they have never been. The Apostle Paul's prayer in

Ephesians 1 contains the necessary ingredients for every Christian to breakthrough any barriers they may face.

That the God of our Lord Jesus Christ, the Father of glory, may give unto you the spirit of wisdom and revelation in the knowledge of him: The eyes of your understanding being enlightened; that ye may know what is the hope of his calling, and what the riches of the glory of his inheritance in the saints, And what is the exceeding greatness of his power to us-ward who believe, according to the working of his mighty power, which he wrought in Christ, when he raised him from the dead, and set him at his own right hand in the heavenly places, Far above all principality, and power, and might, and dominion, and every name that is named, not only in this world, but also in that which is to come: And hath put all things under his feet, and gave him to be the head over all things to the church, Which is his body, the fulness of him that filleth all in all.

Ephesians 1:17-23

The Apostle Paul called this necessary ingredient the spirit of wisdom and revelation. That is the main focus of this prayer and the greatest need of every believer. As Chuck Yeager used the X-1 as the vehicle to break the sound barrier, the spirit of wisdom and revelation is the vehicle that enables believers to see things they have never seen, to go places they have never been, and to receive things they have never received.

Since 1947, the X-1's original breakthrough to the supersonic speed of Mach 1 (700 mph) has revolutionized our flight capabilities. NASA's X-43A scramjet worked successfully at nearly Mach 9.8 (7,000 mph) on November 16, 2004.[3] The original breakthrough in supersonic flight has had an incredible impact on the future.

God wants you to have more than one breakthrough in your life. He wants you to go from Mach 1 to Mach 2 and all the way to Mach 9.8! God wants you to have ever-increasing breakthroughs in revelation.

This prayer in Ephesians is not really asking that God would do something for us, but that we would see what God has already done for us and what already belongs to us in Christ. Paul is praying for a breakthrough in revelation!

BREAKTHROUGH IN REVELATION

The barriers we run into are not because God's plan of redemption is deficient. The real barrier is in our knowledge and understanding of what God has done for us in the death, burial, and resurrection of Christ. We need to see who we are and what we have in Christ. When we live in the light of revelation knowledge, we will not only enjoy the blessings of God, but we will also fulfill the call of God.

Every breakthrough in faith comes from a breakthrough in revelation. Every breakthrough in receiving the blessings of God comes from a breakthrough in revelation and understanding. Every advance in fulfilling the call of God in our lives today comes from a breakthrough in the spirit of wisdom and revelation. The power that is available to us as believers is accessed through the supernatural revelation of God and His Word.

It is possible to be saved and filled with the Holy Ghost and not walk in the abundance Jesus provided for us. It is possible to come to church week after week and remain totally unaware of who we are and what we have in Christ. It is possible to run around the church and shout "Hallelujah!" with tears rolling down our cheeks, and go home sick, depressed, poor, and still defeated in life. It is possible to live far below our authority and privileges as children of God just because we cannot see the truth.

The Ephesians 1 prayer is not for heathens or sinners. Paul was praying for people who had been filled with the Holy Spirit and spoke in tongues. Acts 19:11 tells us that God wrought special miracles by the hands of Paul in Ephesus. They even experienced tremendous revival and phenomenal miracles in their lives and in their church. Historical records even say that the church at Ephesus grew to more than one hundred thousand people! These believers were on fire and within two years all of Asia heard the Word of God (Acts 19:10). Yet, Paul wrote to them and said, "I'm praying for you."

INSPIRATION AND INFORMATION

Brother John Osteen, a Baptist preacher who got hungry for the Holy Spirit, knew there had to be more to experience in his walk with God. So, he started hanging around Full Gospel people. Brother Osteen shared, "The Full Gospel believers scared me the first time I attended their services because they were singing and playing wild music that I was not used to. People started jumping and dancing and running and shouting all over the place. I thought 'My, my, my! What in the world is going on here?' Finally, the service settled down and people went back to their seats. The minister stood up and said, 'Now, we want to pray for all of you who are struggling with depression.' As I watched, many of the same people who had been jumping, dancing, and running now got up and made their way to the front for prayer because they were struggling with depression. I thought, 'My Lord, if they are depressed, I don't have a chance!'"

Full Gospel people tend to have more inspiration than they do information, but faith comes by the information, not just the inspiration of the Word. The Word of God contains supernatural revelation knowledge that is essential for our faith to work properly. It is more than just "feeling the anointing." It is much more than listening to Brother So-and-So sing a moving worship song that caused a tear to roll down our cheeks. You and I need to know who we are and what we have in Christ.

The Holy Spirit inspired Paul to write down this prayer in Ephesians 1, so it must be important for every believer to pray it continually. This also must mean we are not going to receive what is included in this prayer if we do not pray for it. This is not just Paul's prayer for the Ephesian church. This is the prayer of Jesus for every believer.

[1] *Gen. Chuck Yeager and Leo Janos, Yeager (New York, NY: Bantam Books, 1985), p. 130.*

[2] *Ibid: p. 130.*

[3] *John Antczak, "Experimental NASA Jet Aims for Speed Record," Associated Press, http://aolsvc.news.aol.com/news/article.adp?id=20041115025409990001 (accessed November 15, 2004).*

No great preacher has arisen to bless the people of God who has not lighted his torch at the flame kindled by Paul. Whole sermons may be found in separate words: whole volumes in single sentences. Even after nineteen hundred years, Paul is preaching every week in a thousand languages in a hundred thousand pulpits all over the world. Paul's Letters are the advanced teaching of the Lord Jesus Christ.

P.C. Nelson

I ask—ask the God of our Master, Jesus Christ, the God of glory—to make you intelligent and discerning in knowing him personally, your eyes focused and clear, so that you can see exactly what it is he is calling you to do, grasp the immensity of his glorious way of life he has for Christians, oh, the utter extravagance of his work in us who trust him—endless energy, boundless strength! All this energy issues from Christ: God raised him from death and set him on a throne in deep heaven, in charge of running the universe, everything from galaxies to governments, no name and no power exempt from his rule. And not just for the time being, but forever. He is in charge of it all, has the final word on everything. At the center of all this, Christ rules the church. The church, you see, is not peripheral to the world; the world is peripheral to the church. The church is Christ's body, in which he speaks and acts, by which he fills everything with his presence.

Ephesians 1:16-23 (MSG)

4

The Turning Point

REVOLUTION: to effect radical change; the overthrow and replacement of a government or political system; one complete turn in the action of revolving...any fundamental complete change...[1]

REVELATION: a revealing; something revealed; God's manifestation of himself to man; something revealed to man by God...[2]

> *For I neither received it of man, neither was I taught it, but by the revelation of Jesus Christ.*
> *Galatians 1:12*

MARTIN LUTHER'S REFORMATION REVOLUTION

I wonder if Martin Luther realized he was starting a revolution when he nailed his ***Ninety-Five Theses*** to the Wittenberg church door in Germany on October 31, 1517. This one action of Martin Luther was the beginning of the Protestant Reformation. Luther also translated the Bible into German and affected the church world and the entire nation.

After studying the scriptures, including the writings of the Apostle Paul, Martin Luther had a revelation that "the just shall live by faith." He saw things in the Word of God he had never seen before. This revelation caused a revolution in his thinking. By revelation knowledge of the scriptures, he came to the conclusion that salvation was by faith alone—not by works appointed by the church or the sacraments. An excerpt from Eddie L. Hyatt's book *2000 Years of Charismatic Christianity* gives us some insight into Luther's reformation revolution.

...Professor Bengt Hoffman of Lutheran Theological Seminary in Gettysburg, Pennsylvania reports a conversation in which Cochelus asks Luther if he had received special revelations. Luther was silent for a moment, and then replied, "Est mihi revelatum, yes, he had had revelations." It seems that one of these was similar to Paul's experience of being caught up to the third heaven (2 Cor. 12).[3]

Hyatt's book also says this of Luther when he was challenged about his beliefs:

He relied on the revelation of God to him— through the Word, but via the Spirit in a personal manner.[4]

Luther's revelation, that the just shall live by faith, shook the church world and caused a revolution that affects the church world even today.

AZUSA STREET REVOLUTION

Charles Parham and William Seymour had an unquenchable desire for God. Charles Parham studied and traveled to gain an understanding of the move of the Spirit. Hyatt says of Parham:

> *...in his opinion, the church of his day lacked the power necessary to fulfill the mandate of the Great Commission. He yearned for that outpouring from heaven that would make the church a dynamic force in the earth, both in word and in deed.*[5]

In 1906, William Seymour applied to Parham's Bible School. Southern segregation laws posed a number of problems for William Seymour. Parham, nonetheless, skirted the legal restrictions by arranging for Seymour to sit in an adjoining room where, through an open door, he was able to listen to the lectures.[6]

SEYMOUR COULD "SEE MORE"

William Seymour could only see out of one of his eyes. I like to say that he could "see more" with his one eye than most people could see with two because he could see the things of God. In other words, he had a spirit of wisdom and revelation that ultimately led to the Azusa Street revival in 1906. Even with his natural eyesight impaired, his supernatural vision caused a revolution.

In the 1940's God used Oral Roberts in the Healing Revival. Later, Kenneth E. Hagin (Dad Hagin) revolutionized a whole generation of believers with the revelation of how faith works. In the 1960's and 1970's teenagers and young adults started what was known as the Jesus Movement. Anytime there is a revolution, you can be sure that someone has received a revelation from God.

Over and over again, we can see that God is looking for someone who will dare to believe that His Word is true. The men and women who dare to act like the Bible is true have fueled a revolutionary revelation across the centuries and around the world.

REVOLUTIONS AND TURNING POINTS
IN HISTORY

The *U.S. News and World Report* gave this special report on "History's Turning Points" by Daniel Boorstin:

> *The true watersheds of human affairs are seldom spotted quickly amid the tumult of headlines broadcast on the hour. Overfed on the news, we are in danger of having our sense of history polluted by today's headlines. Today more than ever we need to sharpen our vocabulary and remind ourselves of the differences between history and current events, between "revolution" and the kinds of "turning points" that confuse our view of the latest bulletins. Not until the 17th century did the word "revolution" cease to mean only the circular movement of celestial bodies in their orbits and begin to describe the great "commotions" in society. "Turning points" is a much more recent addition to our vocabulary. The phrase was embraced in the mid-19th century as a way of indicating*

a sudden change in the direction of things in motion. To move from the wilderness of news into the paths of history, we must distinguish true turning points from mistaken ones. The authentic turning points we call revolutions had centuries old roots.[7]

I like the words "revolution" and "turning point." The Apostle Paul definitely caused a great commotion in society and impacted history. He caused a sudden change of direction in the early church. He revolutionized the thinking of the early church leaders concerning what happened in the death, burial, and resurrection of Jesus Christ.

Gerald Parshall's article, "The Momentous Mission of the Apostle Paul," from *U.S. News & World Report* explains the impact of one man's revolutionary revelation.

In the middle years of the first century, preachers of many philosophical stripes traveled the sea lanes and cobblestone roads of the eastern Roman Empire. Among them was an indefatigable evangelist in a rough coat and crude sandals who supported himself in his missionary work by making tents. Contemporary historians did not deem him worthy of a single mention, having no inkling of how great a tent maker Paul of Tarsus was. They could not know that he was erecting the theological tent of Christianity, making it broad enough to accommodate all manner of humankind, to girdle the globe and to survive two millenniums as a major force in history. He was arrested and driven from one city after another. He was stoned at least once, beaten with rods three times and in five instances given 39 lashes, a punishment that leaves the back a bloody mess and can cause death. While Paul traveled by foot, by donkey, by horseback and by boat across Asia Minor and Macedonia establishing new congregations, he reinforced his gospel to previous converts with a series of letters that have awed even secular historians. Will Durant called them "among the most forceful and eloquent...in all literature." [8]

The Apostle Paul started a revolutionary revelation that still shapes and changes the world today. From Martin Luther to Azusa Street and to the countless other revolutionary revelations, the Lord Jesus Christ used Paul to revolutionize the thinking and understanding of the leaders of the early church. Paul's letters have endured to influence the church today. P.C. Nelson said, **"No great preacher has arisen to bless the people of God who has not lighted his torch at the flame kindled by Paul.** Whole sermons may be found in separate words: whole volumes in single sentences. Even after nineteen hundred years, Paul is preaching every week in a thousand languages in a hundred thousand pulpits all over the world. Paul's Letters are the advanced teaching of the Lord Jesus Christ." [9]

[1] *www.merriam-webster.com, revolution*

[2] *www.merriam-webster.com, revelation*

[3] *Eddie L. Hyatt, 2000 Years of Charismatic Christianity, p. 74.*

[4] *Ibid: p. 74.*

[5] *Ibid: p. 137.*

[6] *Ibid: p. 143.*

[7] *Daniel J. Boorstin, "History's Hidden Turning Points," U.S. News & World Report, Vol. 11o, No. 15, April 22, 1991, p. 52.*

[8] *Gerald Parshall, "The Momentous Mission of the Apostle Paul,"U.S. News & World Report, Vol. 110, No. 15, April 22, 1991, pp. 54-55.*

[9] *Nelson, P.C. The Life of Paul.*

God is on my side,

For the blood has been applied.

Every need shall be supplied,

Nothing shall be denied.

So I enter into rest,

I know that I am blessed.

I have passed the test,

I will get God's best.

Trina Hankins

...ask the God of our Lord Jesus Christ, the glorious Father, to give you the Spirit, who will make you wise and reveal God to you, so that you will know him. I ask that your minds may be opened to see his light, so that you will know what is the hope to which he has called you, how rich are the wonderful blessings he promises his people, and how very great is his power at work in us who believe. This power working in us is the same as the mighty strength which he used when he raised Christ from death and seated him at his right side in the heavenly world. Christ rules there above all heavenly rulers, authorities, powers, and lords; he has a title superior to all titles of authority in this world and in the next. God put all things under Christ's feet and gave him to the church as supreme Lord over all things. The church is Christ's body, the completion of him who himself completes all things everywhere.

Ephesians 1:17-23 (Good News Bible)

5

The Language of Change

I remember walking through a large cemetery with my dad when I was a little boy. As we walked, I read the inscriptions carved into the different head stones. Along with the names and dates, I also read the comments written about each person. I particularly noticed the word "veteran" on many of the markers. I even commented to my dad about the large number of veterans in the cemetery. My dad just responded, "Yes, there sure are a lot of veterans in this cemetery."

My dad did not realize that I thought a veteran was a veterinarian. We were saying the same word but with two totally different pictures. My dad saw someone who served in the military, but I saw an animal doctor. As a child, I thought it was unusual that so many "dog doctors" could be buried in the same graveyard. I thought, "Wow! So many animal doctors in one cemetery." The town we lived in only had one "dog doctor."

I wondered why so many veterans had died at the same time—maybe they had all been bitten and got rabies. Today, I do know the difference between a veteran and a veterinarian. Even though my dad and I were saying the same thing, we definitely were not seeing the same thing. Effective communication must involve both seeing and saying.

NEW SOUND, NEW SCENERY

Human speech is a characteristic of man made in the image of God. We can see from Genesis 1 that God said and God saw. Sound came before sight in the order of this world's creation. God said and God saw. Everything we can see was made from sound. Sound changes sight. "For we walk by faith and not by sight," 2 Corinthians 5:7. Faith has a certain sound. As we speak the word of faith, things change in our lives. Many people would like to see different scenery in their lives—God says to make a different sound first. Jesus said, "Whosoever shall say...he shall have whatsoever he saith" (Mark 11:23).

In the beginning, a language existed that perfectly expressed the essence of all possible things. The language spoken in the Garden of Eden must have been such a language. In Genesis 11, we can see the power of language from the story of the Tower of Babel. Nothing was impossible when there was unity of language. Because of man's fallen condition and man's capacity to wrongly use this power, God confused the language.

Today, in the language of the Gospel, there is even greater power available. God has redeemed us by the blood of Jesus and has given us the language of redemption in Christ Jesus. God has restored all power to us "in Christ." We are still learning to understand and to speak this new language. It is a language of authority that will move mountains as Jesus said in Mark 11:23. It is a language of healing that Paul spoke in Acts 14:7-10. It is a language of love that Paul described in 1 Corinthians 13. It is the perfect language.

God wants us to learn the language of faith. Language includes reading and comprehension. It also involves communicating through sound. The spirit of wisdom and revelation and the spirit of faith work together for the will of God to be accomplished in us and through us. God communicates to us through His Word. He wants us to see the same thing He sees and say the same thing He says.

In other words, it does not matter what the devil has done in your life. Through the cross of Jesus Christ, there is another language God wants to teach you—the language of redemption, restoration, and freedom. If you can dare to speak this new language, "By Jesus' stripes I was healed," He restores your dominion. Dare to speak "Christ has redeemed me from the curse of the law. I know I have eternal life. I am a child of God because of what Jesus has done!"

THE LANGUAGE OF REDEMPTION

Paul prayed for believers to see what God sees. He prayed that we would see different scenery by the spirit of wisdom and revelation. He prayed that we would have a revolutionary revelation—that we would see things so differently that it would totally change the course of our lives.

The Gospel of Christ is a language of power. It is the power of God working in this world. As believers, we must understand the language of redemption and effectively speak it. We must boldly say, "I am who God says I am. I have what God says I have. I can do what God says I can do!" The Gospel of Christ is a language of power, love, faith, victory, and blessing.

The language of faith or the language of redemption gives us access to the supernatural—we can think like God, see like God, talk like God, and walk with God. Many times people are trying to walk with God. They may actually be saying the same words God says, but they do not see the same picture.

To effectively communicate what God has done for us in Christ we must watch what we say. We must see the same thing God sees. As our eyes are opened to the limitless possibilities of God's plan for our lives, the inheritance that belongs to us in Christ, and the authority we have in Christ, we can see and say the same thing God sees and says about us.

When you speak like God speaks, you will overthrow and overturn anything the devil has done in your life. Speaking the language of redemption will cause a radical change in your thinking and in your seeing. God's Word spoken by your mouth will replace what Satan has told you. Instead of seeing yourself as a failure, you begin to speak God's Word. You speak that you are an overcomer and that you have been seated with Christ in heavenly places. You are a winner in Christ!

You replace what other people have said about you with what God says about you. As you speak the Word of God, the perfect language, there will be a total change in the way you see yourself. The revelation of who you are in Christ will swallow up anything else that has happened to you.

You used to say, "I'm depressed, broke, sick, confused, and beat up by life." Now, you say what God says about you—you speak the perfect language of redemption. "I have joy. I am blessed. I am healed. I know the hope of His calling. I know I have an inheritance in Christ. Jesus has given me authority over the devil!"

Instead of being controlled by the influences of the world, the flesh, and the devil, speaking the perfect language will cause a revolution—a radical change—

in your life. This revolutionary revelation of who you are in Christ will replace how you used to see yourself.

TURN AROUND

A revolution is a turn around. The revelation is causing things to turn around for you right now!

> *When the Lord turned again the captivity of Zion, we were like them that dream. Then was our mouth filled with laughter, and our tongue with singing: then said they among the heathen, The Lord hath done great things for them.*
> *Psalm 126:1, 2*

> *Thou hast turned for me my mourning into dancing: thou hast put off my sackcloth, and girded me with gladness; To the end that my glory may sing praise to thee, and not be silent. O Lord my God, I will give thanks unto thee for ever.*
> *Psalm 30:11, 12*

> *And the Lord turned the captivity of Job and*
> *restored his fortunes, when he prayed for his*
> *friends; also the Lord gave Job twice as much*
> *as he had before.*
> *Job 42:10*

Rejoice now! God has turned your captivity. The revolution has begun. Rejoicing and celebrating is appropriate. Look the enemy in the face and laugh!

The important thing is not to stop questioning. Curiosity has its own reason for existing. One cannot help but be in awe when one contemplates the mysteries of eternity, of life, of the marvelous structure of reality. It is enough if one tries merely to comprehend a little of this mystery every day.

Albert Einstein

May the God of our Lord Jesus Christ, the Father all glorious, give you a spirit that grasps principles [and receives] God's revelation in the sphere of [or, as regards] full knowledge of himself; the eyes of your understanding being enlightened to know what is the object of our hope to which he has called us, what the wealth of the glory of his heritage in God's people, and what the transcendent greatness of his power in relation to us believers, as seen in the operation of the might of his strength, which he set in operation in Christ by raising him from the dead and seating him on his right hand in the heavenly regions, above every [Angelic] Ruler and [Heavenly] Authority, [Celestial] Power and Lord, above every name that is invoked whether in this age or the age to come. [God] has set all things under his feet, and appointed him supreme head of the church, his body; [Christ] the fulness of him who fills the universe completely.

Ephesians 1:17-23 (Hudson)

6

Seeing the Unseen

...this prayer is one for further light and increased understanding on your part, that the God of our Lord Jesus Christ, the Father of all glory, may give you the spiritual wisdom and revelation, which are found in the clear full knowledge of Him...and illuminate your inner vision, the eyes of your heart, thereby explaining and opening to you the full nature of his calling and its aim and expectation, revealing too what an abundance of glory is implied in this inheritance in the saints.

Ephesians 1:17, 18 (Cornish)

Launched by NASA in 1990, the Hubble Telescope revolutionized the study of our universe. Many mysteries of our universe have been revealed by the Hubble's discoveries. However, with all we are coming to understand about the universe, there is still so much more to be discovered.

The new and dramatic discoveries of the Hubble are possible because a Space Shuttle mission launched Hubble into a low-Earth orbit 600 kilometers above the ground. This orbit above Earth's atmosphere allows the Hubble to see things more clearly. Just before light arrives at the telescope mirrors on Earth, it must travel through our turbulent atmosphere. Earth's atmosphere blurs the fine cosmic details. This same turbulence in our atmosphere makes stars appear to twinkle on a dark night. By putting the Hubble Telescope in space, NASA found a way to avoid the problem of Earth's turbulent atmosphere.

Hubble's orbit above the Earth's distorting atmosphere allows scientists to see and observe things very clearly. The Hubble has been able to see galaxies 12 billion light years away and has even captured images of new stars being born.

Because it has been launched far above Earth's atmosphere, Hubble can detect light with "eyes" five times sharper than the best ground telescopes. The Hubble is able to "see" deep into space where some of the most profound mysteries have before remained unseen. Chet Raymo said:

> *Through our science we have created magnificent spacecrafts and telescopes to explore the night and the light and the half light. We have made visible things that are invisible to the unaided eye. We have brought the dreamy heavens down to Earth, held them in the mind's eye. Our explorations have produced a vast archive of remarkable astronomical images....*
>
> *The riches are too many for choices, the revelations beautiful and dreadful. Who can look at these images and not be transformed? The heavens declare God's glory.* [1]

FOCUSED AND CLEAR

...your eyes focused and clear, so that you can
see exactly what it is he is calling you to do,
grasp the immensity of this glorious way of life
he has for his followers.
Ephesians 1:18 (MSG)

In Ephesians 1, the Apostle Paul described the spirit of wisdom and revelation as the "eyes of your understanding being enlightened." The spirit of wisdom and revelation make it possible for us to see the mystery or unseen realities of our redemption.

In Christ we have been launched into heavenly places to be able to clearly see God's plans and purposes. We can see a clearer picture of what God sees when we have a spirit of wisdom and revelation.

And hath raised us up together, and made us sit
together in heavenly places in Christ Jesus.
Ephesians 2:6

By the spirit of wisdom and revelation we can see things from the perspective of what God has done for us in Christ. We can rise above the turbulent atmosphere of our experiences. We can see the picture of who we are and what we have in Christ.

SEE THE UNSEEN

God wants to open a different set of eyes so you can see the unseen. The unseen is no less real than the seen. We can rise above the turbulent atmosphere of our past experiences. The unseen is actually more real than the seen because everything that you can see came out of the unseen.

> *While we look not at the things which are seen,*
> *but at the things which are not seen: for the*
> *things which are seen are temporal; but the*
> *things which are not seen are eternal.*
> *2 Corinthians 4:18*

When you look at 2 Kings, you can see an example of being able to see the unseen. In the Old Testament, a prophet was called a "seer" because he didn't just see what everyone else saw. He could see what everyone else could not see.

In 2 Kings 6, Elisha was "seeing" and knew what the enemy was going to do before they ever went to battle. The king of Israel won every battle because Elisha could see where the enemy was planning to attack before they moved.

One morning Elisha's servant woke up, pulled back the curtains, and suddenly realized he was in a threat environment. The Bible says the mountains were filled with enemy soldiers that had surrounded them. They wanted to kill Elisha because he told the king of Israel everything they were planning.

The servant, full of fear, ran in to wake up Elisha. "We're gonna die today! They're gonna kill us. Wake up! Get up! We're gonna die."

Elisha answered his servant, ***"Fear not: for they that be with us are more than they that be with them,"*** 2 Kings 6:16. The servant must have looked at Elisha like he was crazy. "Now, where did you learn arithmetic? They that be with us are more than they that be with them? There are only two of us and hundreds of troops surrounding us! How can they that be with us be more than they that be with them?"

Elisha prayed for his servant. He did not pray, "Oh, God, just help my servant to be more dedicated.

He's just not dedicated enough. Lord, just help him to die right now like a real soldier." He did not pray, "Oh, God, we need you to do something! God, show up or it's all over right now!"

The prophet prayed the same prayer as Ephesians 1. He said, *"Lord, I pray for you to open his eyes that he may see...,"* 2 Kings 6:17. The stressed out servant said, "My eyes are open. Can't you see my eyes are open?" The prophet said, "Yeah, but you need some glasses."

When Elisha prayed, "Lord open his eyes," the servant saw the same thing that Elisha saw. He saw that God had sent angels and chariots of fire that surrounded Elisha and surrounded the army. There was no reason to be afraid.

Even with his natural eyes open, the servant lacked the power of supernatural vision. The prophet of God in those days was called a "seer" because the Spirit of God gave him supernatural vision. The seer prayed for the non-seer and his eyes were opened. When his vision was changed, everything was changed.

MYSTERIES EXPLAINED

The entire Bible is actually written from the spirit of wisdom and revelation. Creation would still be a mystery today if Moses had not written the book of Genesis. How could Moses have written Genesis 1? How did he know what happened? He obviously was not there. God must have opened the eyes of his understanding. The only way Moses could have known is by the spirit of wisdom and revelation. Through the spirit of wisdom and revelation, Moses saw the mystery of creation.

In Exodus 33, Moses prayed, "God, show me your glory." God answered, "I will make all of my goodness pass before thee." We know from Genesis 1 that God is the creator of all good. You can see that God spoke, and then God saw that "it was good." As the goodness of God passed by, maybe this is when Moses' spiritual eyes, the eyes of his understanding, were opened or enlightened.

He saw by the spirit of wisdom and revelation exactly what happened when God created the heavens and the earth. Imagine Moses' reaction when he began to see what happened at creation. "Whoa! Let

me write this down!" Moses saw and wrote the book
of Genesis by the spirit of wisdom and revelation.

X-RAY VISION

*I pray that the God of our Lord Jesus Christ, the
all-glorious Father, may give you the spiritual
powers of wisdom and vision, by which there
comes the knowledge of him. I pray that your
inward eyes may be illumined, so that you may
know what is the hope to which he calls you,
what the wealth and glory of the share he offers
you among his people in their heritage....*
Ephesians 1:16-18 (NEB)

The Apostle Paul saw something by the spirit of
wisdom and revelation that was even greater than
what Moses saw in Genesis 1. Paul's letters are even
different from the four Gospels. Matthew, Mark,
Luke, and John are a photograph of redemption.
Paul's letters are an x-ray.

If you saw an x-ray of a person you knew, you
might not even recognize who it is. In a photograph,
you see a person. An x-ray is the same person, but it is

a different kind of picture. In the four Gospels, you see what man saw in the death, burial, and resurrection of Christ. You see a photograph.

Paul's letters show us an x-ray of the death, burial, and resurrection of Christ—same picture, same event, but a different kind of picture. Paul shows us what God saw. Paul saw what happened in the Spirit, not just what happened to Christ, but what happened "in Christ." God saw us there in Christ. We died with Him, were buried with Him, and were made alive with Him. We were also raised up together with Him.

Paul was not physically there for the death, burial, and resurrection of Christ, but he wrote about what happened by revelation knowledge. Remember that the entire Bible is written revelation. It must be possible for every believer to experience this same revelation because Paul prayed for believers to know the ***"exceeding greatness of his power which he wrought in Christ, when he raised him from the dead...,"*** Ephesians 1:19, 20.

The words in the Bible are spiritual revelation that describe spiritual or unseen realities and explain the mystery of your redemption. You can read the Bible with just your intellect and read it like a regular book, or you can allow the Holy Spirit to open up revelation to you.

Dad Hagin said to pray the prayer in Ephesians 1 every day for at least six months. He said the first thing that will happen is that the Bible will become a different book to you. The Bible is really the recording of God, who is a Spirit. You can literally walk right into the Bible, and the Word of God can literally walk right into you.

DON'T LET THE DEVIL OUTBLUFF YOU

...I pray for you constantly, asking God, the glorious Father of our Lord Jesus Christ, to give you wisdom to see clearly and really understand who Christ is and all that he has done for you.
Ephesians 1:16-17 (TLB)

I don't understand a whole lot about the game of poker, but I happened to see the world championship on TV one day and decided to watch for a few minutes. I watched long enough to see them play a few hands. In just a matter of minutes, I watched hundreds of thousands of dollars change among the players.

While they were playing, the cameras showed the television audience the exact hand each player had. The funny thing I noticed was that the player who won, beat the player with the better hand. The player with the better hand folded because the other player outbluffed him. I thought, "Now isn't that something? One guy had the better hand, but the other guy bluffed him even though he had a losing hand."

The mystery of what the other player had in his hand was revealed to me by the television camera. I could see who really had the winning hand. Everything God has done for us in Christ belongs to us. Yet, many times we fold and throw in the cards even though we're holding the winning hand. We don't understand the mystery of our redemption in Christ. We think, "Well, I wonder what the other side has." The other side doesn't have anything. Christ has already dethroned and defeated the devil!

You need the spirit of wisdom and revelation so you can see what God has already done for you in Christ. The mystery of your redemption can be explained by the spirit of wisdom and revelation.

Understanding who you are and what you have in Christ is covered more in depth in my books *Taking Your Place In Christ* and *The Power of Identification With Christ.*

[1] *Chet Raymo, Skeptics and True Belivers*

The final mystery is oneself. When one has weighed the sun in the balance, and measured the steps of the moon, and mapped out the seven heavens star by star, there still remains oneself. Who can calculate the orbit of his own soul?

Oscar Wilde
De Profundis

Psalm 8:3-6
1 Corinthians 2:9-14

*That the God of our Lord Jesus Christ, the Father of the glory,
might give to you a spirit of wisdom and revelation in the sphere
of a full knowledge of Him, the eyes of your heart being in an
enlightened state with a view to your knowing the hope of His
calling, what is the wealth of the glory of His inheritance in
the saints, and what is the super abounding greatness of His
inherent power to us who are believing ones as measured by
the operative energy of the manifested strength of His might,
which might was operative in the Christ when He raised Him
from among the dead and seated Him at His right hand in
the heavenly places, over and above every government and
authority and power and lordship and every name that is
constantly being named, not only in this age, but also in the
one about to come. And all things He put in subjection under
His feet, and Him He gave as Head over all things to the
Church, which is of such a nature as to be His body, the fulness
of the One who constantly is filling all things with all things.*

Ephesians 1:17-23 (Wuest)

7

Unlimited Possibilities

In 1947 Captain Charles E. "Chuck" Yeager piloted the X-1 to a speed of Mach 1.06 (700 mph) and became the first person to fly faster than the speed of sound.

As I mentioned earlier in this book, over 50 years later in March of 2004, NASA launched an experimental jet that reached a speed of nearly 5,000 mph. This record breaking speed, however, did not satisfy NASA. NASA's third and last X-43A scramjet blasted into the record books just a few months later as it flew at nearly Mach 9.8 (7,000 mph). [1]

The sound barrier Chuck Yeager broke on that October morning is still being broken today at an exponential rate. Scientists may use scramjet technology to develop hypersonic missiles and airplanes or reusable space launch vehicles. These devices would have a potential for offering speeds of at least Mach 15.[2] All of these breakthroughs in technology go back to that day when Chuck Yeager broke the sound barrier in his X-1 jet.

On April 25, 2005, the Hubble Space Telescope celebrated its fifteenth year of service in space. Steve Maran, author of Astronomy for Dummies said, "Hubble has been arguably the greatest telescope of all time." [3]

The Hubble has made major discoveries in every area of astronomy. Astronomer Bruce Margon of the Space Telescope Science Institute in Baltimore, which manages Hubble for NASA said, "The amazing thing about Hubble is that it is a frontline scientific instrument that grows stronger every year." [4]

Margon also said, "Hubble's lasting legacy will not be based on astronomical facts, but in the way it has opened up science to the public." [5]

UNLIMITED POSSIBILITIES

Every breakthrough in faith comes from a breakthrough in revelation knowledge, not necessarily new information. Lester Sumrall once said that most Christians never progress beyond their initial revelation of God. You cannot go forward in faith without going forward in revelation.

The spirit of wisdom and revelation opens our eyes to see the unlimited possibilities of God. After 30 years of teaching, preaching, and evangelizing the world, the Apostle Paul expressed his continuing personal desire for a deeper revelation of Jesus Christ.

That I may know him, and the power of his resurrection....
Philippians 3:10

[For my determined purpose is] that I may know Him [that I may progressively become more deeply and intimately acquainted with Him, perceiving and recognizing the wonders of His Person more strongly and more clearly],

> *and that I may in the same way come to know*
> *the power outflowing from His resurrection*
> *[which it exerts over believers]....*
>
> *AMP*

The Holy Spirit inspired Paul to write the prayer in Ephesians 1 so it must be important for every born again, Spirit-filled believer to pray it also. That must mean that you will not get the spirit of wisdom and revelation if you don't ask for it. If you are continuing to pray for the spirit of wisdom and revelation, that must also mean that it is progressive; an ever increasing revelation.

Jesus' earth ministry was run on revelation. He said, "I see what my Father does and I do what I see." Today, God wants us to see supernaturally. When the eyes of our heart are opened, we can see, say, and do the will of God.

A breakthrough in revelation enables us to see what God sees. Revelation also changes our perspective. The view is so different when we see things from God's perspective. God sees us in Christ. Everything looks different in the light of our redemption in Christ Jesus.

The way you see, your whole perspective, changes with the spirit of wisdom and revelation. Revelation will revolutionize your dedication to do the will of God. When the eyes of our hearts are flooded with light, great changes will happen in our lives.

...the eyes of your understanding enlightened still more and more; that being thus illuminated, ye may know in a more comprehensive manner than you now do...

Ephesians 1:18 (Doddridge)

In his book, <u>*The Life of St. Paul,*</u> James Stalker says of Jesus:

He had to carry His deepest thoughts out of the world with Him unuttered, trusting with sublime faith that the Holy Spirit would lead His church to grasp them in the course of its subsequent development. [6]

Stalker also says the following about Paul and his writings:

> *The right way to look at them is to regard them*
> *as the continuation of Christ's own teaching.*
> *They contain the thoughts that Christ carried*
> *away from the earth with Him unuttered.* [7]

Paul, by the Holy Spirit, had a revelation of the death, burial, and resurrection of Jesus Christ. There is power in revelation knowledge. The Apostle Paul prayed for believers to have a spirit of wisdom and revelation in the knowledge of God. Revelation is not something you see with your natural eyes or learn by head or sense knowledge. Revelation comes when the eyes of your heart, your spiritual eyes, are opened.

We live in this world, but we are not of this world. We are tempted to walk by sight, but we are not just regular people who live by only what we can see. We walk by faith—by revelation knowledge. Revelation is revealed by the Holy Spirit. Our natural eyes can't see it, but our hearts can see it. We can experience revolutionary revelation given by Jesus from the Father by the Holy Spirit.

EVER INCREASING

God created you to know that there is more than what you have right now—there is more available. He's looking for somebody that will believe God. While everyone else is scared, God is looking for someone that will act in faith. He's looking for somebody who will know God (Daniel 11:32).

If you want life to be different for you, take this prayer in Ephesians 1 and pray it everyday for at least 6 months. If you only pray it once a week, you don't really want life to be different. If you do want life to be different, then pray this prayer everyday. If you really want to know what the will of God is, if you really want to be in the right place at the right time with the right people, if you really want to be led by the Spirit, take this prayer and pray it. Believe God for a breakthrough in revelation.

Believe for a revolutionary revelation in your understanding, in the eyes of your heart. Believe for a breakthrough in the way you see yourself, the way you see the call of God, the way you see your inheritance and the way you see your authority as a believer.

[1] *NASA-Hypersonic X-43A Takes Flight,* http://www.nasa.gov/missions/research/x43-main.html (accessed November 30, 2004).

[2] John Antczak, "Experimental NASA Jet Aims for Speed Record," Associated Press, November 15, 2004, http:// aolsvc.news.aol.com/ news /article.adp?id =2004111502 54 09990001 (accessed November 15, 2004).

[3] Vergano, Dan. 2005. NASA's Bright Star, Hubble Turns 15. USA TODAY.com, March 25, 2005. http:// aolsvc. news.aol.com / news /article. adp ?id =200 504 250 70609990009.

[4] Ibid.

[5] Ibid.

[6] The Life of Saint Paul. James Stalker, p. 15.

[7] Ibid: p. 16.

That the God of our Lord Jesus Christ, the all-glorious Father,
may give you the spiritual powers of wisdom and vision, by
which there comes the knowledge of him. I pray that your inward
eyes may be illumined, so that you may know what is the hope
to which he calls you, what the wealth and glory of the share
he offers you among his people in their heritage, and how vast
the resources of his power open to us who trust in him. They
are measured by his strength and the might which he exerted in
Christ when he raised him from the dead, when he enthroned
him at his right hand in the heavenly realms, far above all
government and authority, all power and dominion, and any
title of sovereignty that can be named, not only in this age but in
the age to come. He put everything in subjection beneath his feet,
and appointed him as supreme head to the church, which is his
body and as such holds within it the fullness of him who himself
receives the entire fullness of God.

Ephesians 1:17-23 (NEB)

8

Find Yourself in the Word

I have always been inspired by the challenge of climbing to the top of Mount Everest. The first people to successfully make it to the top were Sir Edmund Hillary and Tenzing Norgay in 1953. Since they broke that barrier, over 700 people have climbed to the "top of the world."

If you want to climb to the top of Mount Everest, you cannot just take a weekend and make it to the top. If someone were to try it, they would die because it is physically impossible for the body to adjust to the thin air or the lack of oxygen in a short period of time.

The process of climbing the world's tallest mountain takes about three months. During this time, climbers go from lower altitude camps to higher camps, gradually making the ascent. Sometimes they must stay at high altitude camps for as long as three weeks until their bodies adjust to the higher altitude.

At every altitude camp, something happens in their blood. Red blood cells begin to increase because of the lack of oxygen. By the time they reach the final altitude camp, the red blood cells in their bodies have actually doubled in number to be able to carry enough oxygen to keep them alive. Something has to change in your blood for you to survive this kind of mountain climbing.

As I watched the video about Mount Everest, I thought of Psalm 24:3, 4: ***"Who shall ascend into the hill of the Lord? or who shall stand in his holy place? He that hath clean hands, and a pure heart...."*** The Knox translation says, ***"Who dares climb the mountain of the Lord...."***

In these verses, God is giving a challenge to anyone who wants to move up higher in their fellowship with Him. After He gives the condition of clean hands and a pure heart, He gives the promise of "receiving the blessing from the Lord."

There are some blessings you cannot receive from God at "sea level." Every breakthrough in faith comes from a breakthrough in revelation. You will have to move up in revelation and in faith to move up higher into God's presence. The red blood cells of your faith can double so you can move up higher in blessing and fruitfulness in the kingdom of God.

WHERE FAITH BEGINS

Revelation knowledge is where faith actually begins. You can get a giant book on systematic theology and study the Bible from a theological point of view. You can study the Bible from a historical perspective, finding out the time frame, the author, and the setting in which each book of the Bible was written. You can also study the Bible from a geographical point of view, looking at the audience to whom the book was written and the area of the world where they lived. Finally, you can study the Bible from a doctrinal perspective, searching out the major emphasis or theme in a particular book of the Bible.

However, for the spirit of wisdom and revelation to work in your life, you will have to get beyond the theological, the historical, the geographical, and the doctrinal perspectives of the Bible. You will have to enter the realm of the inspirational, where the Bible is God talking to you. In 2 Timothy 3:16, it says that all scripture is inspired, or God–breathed. When the spirit of wisdom and revelation is released in your life, you enter a realm of revelation knowledge where God breathes His Word into your spirit and talks to you personally.

That is when the Word of God comes alive in your life. No longer is Paul talking to only the Ephesian believers in 50 AD—now, God is talking to you! Through the spirit of wisdom and revelation, you begin to find yourself in the Word of God.

JESUS FOUND HIMSELF IN THE WORD

As a child, Jesus not only grew up physically, but He increased in the knowledge of God and the scriptures. When His parents discovered Him missing on their trip home from the temple, they found Him in the temple, hearing and astounding the doctors with his answers.

And the child grew, and waxed strong in spirit, filled with wisdom: and the grace of God was upon him. And Jesus increased in wisdom and stature, and in favour with God and man.

Luke 2:40, 52

He found Himself in this scripture: ***"Then said I, Lo, I come: in the volume of the book it is written of me, I delight to do thy will, O my God: yea, thy law is within my heart,"*** Psalm 40:7-8. The volume of the book contains Him. Hebrews 10:7 also refers to this same verse in reference to sanctifying Himself to do God's will. Jesus found His destiny and His substitutionary work in the scriptures.

JESUS DECLARED WHO HE WAS

Jesus was bold about saying what the scriptures said about Him. Luke 4 tells how Jesus returned to Galilee in the power of the Spirit after overcoming the temptations of the devil in the wilderness. He went to the temple, took the Book and found Himself in the scriptures Isaiah had written hundreds of years before. That day there was a fulfillment of Isaiah's ancient prophecy. Through a revolutionary revelation, Jesus Christ found Himself in Isaiah 61:1, 2.

> *And there was delivered unto him the book of the prophet Esaias. And when he had opened the book, he found the place where it was written, The Spirit of the Lord is upon me, because he hath anointed me to preach the gospel to the poor; he hath sent me to heal the brokenhearted, to preach deliverance to the captives, and recovering of sight to the blind, to set at liberty them that are bruised, To preach the acceptable year of the Lord. And he closed the book, and he gave it again to the minister, and sat down. And the eyes of all them that were in the synagogue were fastened on him. And he began to say unto them, This day is this scripture fulfilled in your ears.*
> *Luke 4:17-21*

The anointing of the Holy Spirit upon Jesus gave Him the revelation that Isaiah's prophecy was about Him and it was being fulfilled now. He found Himself in the Book and by revelation said, "That's me!" At that moment, His public ministry began.

Everything Jesus did in His earth ministry, He did by revelation knowledge. In fact, He said, *"Verily, verily, I say unto you, The Son can do nothing of himself, but what he seeth the Father do: for what things soever he doeth, these also doeth the Son likewise,"* John 5:19.

Jesus fulfilled the scriptures continuously in His earth ministry. For example, as He healed the sick, it was a fulfillment of Isaiah's prophecy (Matthew 8:17).

Today, we find our identity and destiny in the scriptures as we meditate on who we are in Christ. We can find ourselves in Christ, we are made alive with Him and seated with Him, sharing His authority and ministry. We then can walk in the same footsteps of faith by following His example of living a life of obedience to God's plan (1 Peter 2:21, Romans 4:12). He said, *"My Father worketh hitherto, and I work,"* John 5:17. Every time Jesus acted on the Word revealed to Him, it changed everything. When you find yourself in the Word, get ready for a breakthrough in the will of God for your life.

Every breakthrough in faith comes through a

breakthrough in revelation. The moment you receive the Word as God talking to you is the moment you begin to act like the Bible is true. When Paul says, "My God shall supply all your need," you forget about the Philippian church or the year that letter was written. You say, "This is God talking to me! I receive the Word. He is meeting all my needs according to His riches in glory by Christ Jesus," (Philippians 4:19). A breakthrough in revelation has produced a breakthrough in your faith. This scripture is now God's personal promise to you.

The devil wants to limit you by keeping you in the flesh and in mental reasoning. Revelation is the difference between mental assent and faith. People in mental assent may rattle off the same words, but faith gets results. Faith moves mountains and changes things. Faith brings the money in. Faith causes the supernatural to manifest. Revelation is the key that activates faith.

Moving up in faith is a greater challenge than climbing Mount Everest. With the spirit of wisdom and revelation, we can know the limitless possibilities of God's plan and purpose for our lives. With each new revelation, the Holy Spirit will guide us to another altitude camp. We may have to stay there until our "faith cells" double, but after they double, we can move up higher. The Holy Spirit is our guide, and He will take us to the top if we will listen to Him and follow Him. See you at the top!

THE RICHES OF HIS GLORY

...that the God and Father of our Lord Jesus Christ, who is also the Father of glory, of which he is eternally and immutably possessed, from whom all glory proceeds, and to whom it returns, would give you more abundant supplies of the spirit of wisdom and revelation, to fill you with a more enlarged knowledge of his will, and animate you to the further exercise of every grace in the acknowledgement of him. And in particular, that by his influence and teaching he [would give you] to have the eyes of your understanding enlightened still more and more; that, being thus illuminated, ye may know, in a more comprehensive manner than you now do, what is the great and important hope of his calling, what are the high conceptions you

should have of that excellent object which the gospel proposes to your pursuit, and with what certainty and delight you should look forward to it, and may discern more fully what are the inexpressible advantages, and what the glorious riches and inestimable treasures, of his inheritance in the saints, which he distributes with so liberal a hand among them in the blessings of his grace at present, in consequence of having adopted them to himself, and which hereafter they shall possess in perfect happiness and glory, and shall for ever enjoy with him and with each other. And that you may be thus more thoroughly sensible what [is] the exceeding greatness of his power which he hath manifested in the operations of this grace towards us who cordially believe his gospel, according to the energy of the power of his might, influencing our hearts in such a manner, as effectually to conquer all our prejudices against Christianity, and against true religion in every form. This is indeed a power, like that which is the confirmation of our faith, as being the authentic seal of the gospel, set to it by that energy which he exerted in his Son Jesus Christ, when he lay a cold and mangled corpse in the sepulchre, in raising him from the dead, and thus declaring him to be the Son of God with power, and by which too he seated [him] at his own right hand in heavenly [places,] in the possession of the highest dignity and glory; having exalted him far above all the ranks in the angelic world, even above every principality, and power, and might, and dominion, however they are distinguished in the celestial hierarchy, and above every name, how honourable soever, that is named, or had in any account, not only in this world, but also in that which is to come; so that there never has been, and never shall be, among all the inhabitants of heaven or earth, any one so dear and excellent, so high and honourable, in the sight of God as he is. And it is delightful to pursue the meditation; reflecting farther, that the Divine power hath not only invested our ascended Saviour with supreme dignity, but likewise with universal authority; and hath subjected all things whatsoever under his feet, that he may overrule and manage them as he will, and given him [to be] supreme Head over all things to the church, for its protection, benefit, and advantage. Even that church which is his body, and which as such is ever dear and precious to him, and, being made complete in him, is regarded as the fulness of him who filleth all persons in all places with all kind of good things which they possess, and yet delights in this as his chosen dwelling, even as an holy temple which he hath consecrated to himself.

Ephesians 1:17-23 (Doddridge)

SECTION TWO:
REVOLUTIONARY REVELATIONS

Everyone takes the limits of his own vision for the limits of the world.

Arthur Schopenhauer

I pray that your minds may be so enlightened that you may know what the hope is to which he calls you, the glorious wealth which he invites you to share with all his people, and the limitless scope of his power at work in us once we believe in him. This is that same stupendous power which he exerted when he raised Christ from death and enthroned him at his right hand in the supernatural world. There he rules supreme over every ruler, authority, power and lordship, high above every title that can be named not only in this age but in the age to come. And God has put all things under his feet and has given him to the church as its supreme head. The church is his body, and when the body joins the head then he who completes all things will be himself completed.

Ephesians 1:17-23 (Translators New Testament)

9

You Can Know

[For I always pray to] the God of our Lord Jesus Christ, the Father of glory, that He may grant you a spirit of wisdom and revelation [of insight into mysteries and secrets] in the [deep and intimate] knowledge of Him, By having the eyes of your heart flooded with light, so that you can know and understand the hope to which He has called you, and how rich is His glorious inheritance in the saints (His set-apart ones), And [so that you can know and understand] what is the immeasurable and unlimited and

> *surpassing greatness of His power in and for us*
> *who believe....*
> *Ephesians 1:17-19 (AMP)*

In Ephesians 1, Paul prayed for believers to know three things specifically through the spirit of wisdom and revelation knowledge: the hope of His calling, the riches of the glory of His inheritance in the saints, and the exceeding greatness of His power to those who believe.

The spirit of wisdom and revelation is necessary and mandatory to access the call, the inheritance, and the authority we have as believers. To know and understand these three things requires that believers have the eyes of their understanding (of their hearts) enlightened or flooded with light so they can see things differently. The reason this prayer is so important to believers is that the call of God, the inheritance, and the authority of the believer must be accessed supernaturally.

The spirit of wisdom and revelation helps believers see themselves the way that God sees them. When you see yourself the way that God sees you, you not only see what God has done for you in Christ, but you also see everything that is available and belongs to you because of what God has already done for you in Christ.

THE HOPE OF HIS CALLING

...and illuminate your inner vision, the eyes of your heart, thereby explaining and opening to you the full nature of his calling and its aim and expectation...
Ephesians 1:18 (Cornish)

The moment you are born again in Christ, you possess a supernatural calling and identity in your spirit. That is why it takes the spirit of wisdom and revelation to open the eyes of your heart to access who you are and what God has called you to do.

Before I formed thee in the belly I knew thee; and before thou camest forth out of the womb I sanctified thee, and I ordained thee a prophet unto the nations. Then said I, Ah, Lord God! behold, I cannot speak: for I am a child. But the Lord said unto me, Say not, I am a child:

> *for thou shalt go to all that I shall send thee,*
> *and whatsoever I command thee thou shalt*
> *speak. Be not afraid of their faces: for I am*
> *with thee to deliver thee, saith the Lord. Then*
> *the Lord put forth his hand, and touched my*
> *mouth. And the Lord said unto me, Behold I*
> *have put my words in thy mouth.*
> *Jeremiah 1:4-9*

God told Jeremiah, "I called you before you were ever born. Now, let me tell you who you are. Don't say you are something different. Say that you are who I say that you are." Notice that God touched Jeremiah's mouth. For Jeremiah to fulfill the call of God on his life, he could not speak or see himself just "naturally." God told Jeremiah to say he was who God said he was. Anytime God wants to change someone's life, He always touches their mouth.

Each one of us has a call of God on our lives. Each of us also has a choice. We can function in a lower calling, bumping around in God's permissive will for the rest of our lives, or we can say, "I'm pressing for the high calling of God upon my life" (Philippians 3:14). The high calling will always cost you more than the low calling; however, the high calling will bring far greater rewards.

In 2 Kings 2:9, Elisha told Elijah, "I want a double portion." Elijah told him, "You've asked a hard thing, but if you pay the price, you'll get it. If you want a double portion, it will cost you more." The same is true for believers today. The higher calling will cost you more in obedience, sacrifice, and pursuit, but it is absolutely vital that you access the supernatural call on your life.

It does not matter how much stuff you accumulate or how many fun things you do—you will never be happy in life until you are fulfilling the high calling of God on your life. The natural man will always want to pursue natural pleasures and possessions, but the moment you get born again, you are no longer just a natural man. Now you are a new creation in Christ, a supernatural man. Now God intends for you to live in two worlds—to function in this natural world, but also to operate according to His unseen world. You can only access God's unseen world and your own divine call with the spirit of wisdom and revelation.

THE RICH INHERITANCE

...and what the riches of the glory of his inheritance in the saints.

Ephesians 1:18

There was a certain prosperous grandfather who only had one little granddaughter. When she was born he deposited one million dollars in her account. The little girl runs and plays, completely oblivious about how very rich she is. One day, she will grow up and realize how blessed she is. Then she will be able to receive and enjoy her inheritance that was hers all along. In the same way, when you were born again, the Father God deposited a rich and glorious inheritance in your account. Paul's prayer in Ephesians 1:18 is that the church would have a revelation of this inheritance. He then prays another prayer in Ephesians 3:14-21 and asks God to grant the believer the spiritual strength to grasp the vast love of God and to make a withdrawal from this rich inheritance.

In Romans 8:17, Paul says that you are an heir of God and a joint heir with Jesus Christ. Everything God has belongs to us, and everything Jesus has belongs to us. By the spirit of wisdom and revelation you access the inheritance that is yours through Christ. Paul is not talking about some fluffy little blessings you will enjoy when you get to Heaven. He is talking about enjoying the fullness of God's best blessings right here, right now! As a member of the body of Christ, you have an inheritance to claim that is beyond anything you could ever ask, dream, or imagine.

Growing up as a pastor's kid, my family did not enjoy a luxurious lifestyle by any means. However, I always sensed that God wanted to make me rich. The word "rich" means abundantly provided for. Once I started studying God's Word, I began to get a glimpse of my redemption in Christ. I found out that I had been redeemed from the curse of the law (Galatians 3:13), that the blessing of the Lord makes me rich and adds no sorrow with it (Proverbs 10:22), and that God has made me the head and not the tail (Deuteronomy 28).

I started trying to figure out exactly how God was going to make me rich. I looked at my family and thought, "Maybe someone in my family is going to die and leave me some money." As I looked across my family, I realized a rich inheritance wasn't coming from them.

I was trying to figure out this inheritance that God said belonged to me and how it would happen with my intellect and my mind. I continued to pray the Ephesians 1 prayer:

> *Father God, I'm asking you to give unto me the spirit of wisdom and revelation in the knowledge of God, that the eyes of my understanding would be enlightened so I can know the call of God, the inheritance that belongs to me, and the authority I have as a believer. Give me the spirit of wisdom and revelation in the knowledge of You because I'm not seeing my inheritance clearly. I'm not walking in the light of it. I'm not enjoying my inheritance. The number one thing I need from You is the spirit of wisdom and revelation.*

The Lord spoke to me, "You don't have to wait for somebody rich in your family to die and leave you an inheritance. Actually, someone extremely wealthy in your family has already died and left you everything!"

I told the Lord, "I would sure like to know who that person is." The Lord answered, "His name is

Jesus! He became poor so that through His poverty you might be rich (2 Corinthians 8:9). He also arose from the dead to make sure you received your inheritance. Instead of seeing yourself as a poor person who is trying to prosper, you need to change your perspective and say, 'I am prosperous and my life is changing to line up with who God says I am. I'm not trying to be blessed, I am blessed.'"

My whole perspective on life changed after the Lord spoke those words to me. I began to tell the devil, "You have to take your hands off of my stuff, Satan, because I belong to Jesus. As a believer, I have authority over you. I declare right now that money comes to me. I'm a tither and a giver. I'm blessed coming in and blessed going out. I'm the head and not the tail. I'm going to drive the best, wear the best, live in the best, and eat the best!"

If you found out that you had a wealthy relative who had died and left you millions of dollars in their will, you would conduct some very extensive research to find out how to access your inheritance. Maybe the relative had left you the money years ago, but you never enjoyed the benefits of that inheritance because no one ever told you about it.

Once you found out about your inheritance, you would do everything you could to access what belonged to you. Jesus took our curse so we would no longer be cursed. He paid too high a price for our redemption for us to live on a lower level. We access the inheritance that belongs to us in Christ by the spirit of wisdom and revelation.

> *The Exceeding Greatness of His Power*
> *...the limitless scope of his power at work in us*
> *once we believe in him...*
> *Ephesians 1:19 (Trans)*

In the beginning, God spoke all material substance into being. Electrons began whirling around the nuclei of atoms and the physical creation burst into sight. We know that all matter is made of minute cells of energy called atoms. The tremendous power that holds the protons and neutrons in the center of an atom together has only been understood and demonstrated in the twentieth century. Paul prayed that we would get a revelation of the power released in the resurrection of Christ. The resurrection of Christ was evidently the greatest display of Omnipotence ever set forth, surpassing even that of creation. When God raised up the body of Jesus, the material substance of His body changed so dramatically that from that time on, Jesus had no difficulty walking through solid walls. Somehow the very structure of the atoms of His body were altered. This took tremendous power— even more power than used to create matter in the beginning.

This is what Paul had in mind in his prayer for the Church—not just the power that was loosed in His body in His triumph over physical death, but the power that was unleashed spiritually in His triumph over hell and all its forces. That is the power that is at work in us now! The power that raised Christ from the dead made Him supremely triumphant over hell and all its hosts. Christ's resurrection was more than a triumph over rigor mortis; it was a triumph over all the forces that held us in bondage.

Paul strained his vocabulary in Ephesians 1:19 in an attempt to express what he saw of the might of Christ's resurrection.

And what is the exceeding greatness of his power to us-ward who believe, according to the

> *working of his mighty power.*
>
> *Ephesians 1:19*

There are four different words that Paul used for "power" in an attempt to describe what great power was released in the resurrection of Christ:

> *dunamis = dynamite = ability*
>
> *energia = energy = operative power in exercise*
>
> *kratos = manifested strength*
>
> *ischuos = an endowment of strength*

All four of these words generally mean power. Paul said this "power, power, power, power" that God used to raise Jesus from the dead is not just great but exceeding great. "Exceeding" is the Greek word huperballon, which literally means a throwing beyond.1 Paul said, "This power is great beyond measure, surpassing power, more than enough power."

> *And how very great is his power at work in*
> *us who believe. This power is the same as the*
> *mighty strength which he used when he raised*
> *Christ from death and seated him at his right*

side in the heavenly world.

Ephesians 1:19, 20 (GNB)

...and the limitless scope of his power at work in us once we believe in him. This is the same stupendous power which he exerted when he raised Christ from death and enthroned him at his right hand in the supernatural world.

Translator's New Testament

I pray that you may realize that His power in us who believe, is great beyond all measure. It is the same mighty power that worked in Christ. By that power God raised Him from the dead and had Him sit at His right hand in heaven.

Laubach

...and what the transcendent greatness of His power in us believers as seen in the working of His infinite might when He displayed it in Christ by raising Him from the dead and seating Him at His own right hand in the heavenly realms.

Weymouth

May you experience the incredible outburst of his power in us who rely on his might and his abundant energy. This same energy working in Christ raised him from the dead and gave him spiritual victory and authority over every ruler....
Jordan

Calculate if you can, the gigantic power behind all this...
Carpenter

...the extraordinary power which reacts from him upon all who believe...enormous, overmastering supremacy...
Cornish

...the surpassing greatness of his might in us who believe, as seen in the energy of that resistless might...
Centenary

...incredibly immense strength...
Johnson

...erupting greatness...
Klingensmith

...how overwhelmingly great...
New Berkeley

....incomparably great...
New International Version

...immeasurable...
Noli

...unlimited...
Basic English

Paul saw something awesome. In the revelation that Jesus Christ gave him of His redemptive work—the three days and nights from His death to His resurrection and His ascension to glory—he saw the mighty triumph of Christ. Paul longed for all believers to see this revelation in their own hearts as well.

THE MANHATTAN PROJECT

Paul sounds a lot like the eye witness observers of the first atomic blast in the New Mexico desert July 16, 1945. The bomb was set off at 5:29 a.m. while the sky was still dark. Preliminary calculations had indicated that the explosion should have had the energy of roughly 10,000 tons of TNT. They cautiously gave out the estimations as 5,000 tons. The energy actually released was 20,000 tons, which is small in comparison with today's weapons which are measured in megatons or millions of tons of TNT.

The following excerpts are from the book, <u>Manhattan Project</u>, by Stephane Groueff:

> *Everyone closed his eyes and shielded his face with his hands. The fierce light that followed, almost blinding in spite of their closed eyes, was impossible to describe. There was no frame of reference from anything the observers had experienced before. In a brief moment, the light within twenty miles was equal to several suns at midday. It was seen in Albuquerque,*

Santa Fe, El Paso and other points as far as one hundred eighty miles away. As Brigadier General Farrell wrote later in the report for the Secretary of War, it was "unprecedented, magnificent, beautiful, stupendous and terrifying." Farrell's account, written in the wake of the test, had nothing of the style of a perfunctory military report:

'No man-made phenomenon of such tremendous power had ever occurred before. The lighting effects beggared description. The whole country was lighted by a searing light with the intensity many times that of the midday sun. It was golden, purple, violet, gray, and blue. It lighted every peak, crevasse and ridge of the nearby mountain range with a clarity and beauty that cannot be described but must be seen to be imagined. It was that beauty the great poets dream about but describe most poorly and inadequately. Thirty seconds after the explosion came, first, the air blast pressing hard against people and things, to be followed almost immediately by the strong, sustained, awesome roar which warned of doomsday and made us

feel that we puny things were blasphmous to dare tamper with the forces heretofore reserved to the Almighty. Words are inadequate tools for the job of acquainting those not present with the physical, mental and psychological effects. It had to be witnessed to be realized.' [2]

Those last two sentences sound like Paul in Ephesians 1 when he spoke about the resurrection of Christ.

TIME STOOD STILL

William L. Laurence, a New York Times reporter, wrote the following:

It was like the grand finale of a mighty symphony of the elements; fascinating and terrifying, uplifting and crushing, ominous, devastating, full of great promise and great foreboding.... On that moment hung eternity. Time stood still. Space contracted to a pinpoint. It was as though the earth had opened and the skies split. One felt as though he had been privileged to witness the birth of the world—to be present at the moment of Creation when the Lord said: "Let there be light." ³

Next to Laurence at the twenty-mile observation post was [Dr. Richard] Feynman, [a brash young theoretical physicist with exceptional mathematical talents] who typically, was the only man to disobey the instructions. Ignoring his thick dark glasses, he sat behind the windshield of a car as the whole group nervously tried to establish radio contact with the control post. But central control was so busy that it had forgotten the observers. As the tension mounted, people started adjusting their welder's glasses. "The heck with it!" Feynman muttered. "At twenty miles distance no light could be that bright."

But he was wrong. The tremendous white flash that illumined the desert blinded him for a moment and forced him to turn his head away in pain. Though closed, his eyes saw, as an afterimage, the picture of the explosion in purple. When he opened his eyes a few seconds later, the blinding white light was turning yellow, and a wave of furiously boiling clouds was mounting in the sky. A bright ball of orange flames formed in the air, lighting the clouds with a strange violet glow. There was not a single sound. The spectacle was unfolding in eerie, absolute silence. It lasted about a minute and a half, an incredibly long time during which no one moved, no one said a word. Then, suddenly, there was a sharp, loud blast that tore the desert sky like an immense artillery barrage, followed by thunder rolling back and forth. It came so late that Laurence, surprised, turned to Feynman. "What was that?" he asked, then mumbled, "Oh, that was the bomb we've just been watching..." Feynman himself was shaken by the realization that the blast could reach them with such strength after traveling for an entire minute and a half. [4]

At the five-mile station, two men were knocked down by the blast. The hundred foot steel tower on which the bomb had been placed had completely evaporated, that is, melted to liquid and boiled into vapor at once. The surface sand around the tower for a thousand feet was melted into glass.

RESURRECTION POWER

Paul saw something like this in the Omnipotence exercised by God when He raised Christ from the dead, out of the tomb and raised Him into the heavens. The fact that God used such power shows that there was great resistance to the resurrection and ascension, but to absolutely no avail.

Is the comparison in the natural of an atomic bomb appropriate since it is destructive power? The power of Christ's resurrection is also destructive—not on us, but on the works of the enemy.

> *...For this purpose the Son of God was manifested, that he might destroy the works of the devil.*
> *1 John 3:8*

> *It was to undo all that the devil has done that the Son of God appeared.*
> *The Jerusalem Bible*

...that he might break up the works of the devil.

Young

...that he might put an end to the works of the Evil One.

The Bible in Basic English

...that He should be annulling the acts of the Adversary.

Concordant

Jesus did this in a measure in His earthly ministry, but He came to destroy Satan's works and redeem us primarily through His death and resurrection. In His resurrection, the works of the devil He bore and submitted to as our substitute were ultimately destroyed. The word "destroy" is luo which means to loose, break, or undo. [5] Jesus rose again to undo all that Satan had done in man through the fall. Jesus undid, broke up, put an end to, annulled the works of the devil by first bearing those works in Himself as our substitute in His death, then rising again free from them all. Peter used the word "luo" in 2 Peter 3:10-12:

But the day of the Lord will come as a thief in the night; in the which the heavens shall pass away with a great noise, and the elements shall melt with fervent heat, the earth also and the works that are therein shall be burned up. Seeing then that all these things shall be dissolved, what manner of persons ought ye to be in all holy conversation and godliness, looking for and hasting unto the coming of the day of God, wherein the heavens being on fire shall be dissolved, and the elements shall melt with fervent heat?

2 Peter 3:10-12

Peter used the word "luo" to mean melt and dissolved. When we take this definition back to 1 John 3:8, we get an interesting insight into Christ's destruction of the works of the devil.

Now the Son of God came to the earth with the express purpose of liquidating the devil's activities.

1 John 3:8 (Phillips)

> *The reason the Son of God was made manifest (visible) was to undo (destroy, loosen and dissolve) the works the devil (has done).*
>
> *AMP*

The power that God used to raise Christ from the dead dissolved, melted, and liquidated the works of the devil. It was like that power released in the first atomic bomb that vaporized the tower that supported it. God made Jesus to bear and become all that was wrong with us in spirit, soul, and body and then vaporized it with the power of His resurrection.

Paul saw something like an atomic blast of life, light and power in hell when Jesus was made alive in spirit. He was raised up, re-entered and left the tomb and ascended to Heaven. It was an awesome spectacle, beyond his vocabulary. He longed for all believers to come to see what that power did in Christ and to see that same power was now at work in them.

Like radiation, this resurrection power cannot be seen and is not always felt. It does not always register on our emotions. It is a silent power that we can become conscious of in our spirits, radiating out of the inside of us.

We must get a revelation of that power inside of us, for just as with natural things, we cannot grasp and use them if we cannot see or sense them. Revelation of that power within us and faith activated by our confession of it, puts that power to work in us to duplicate in our souls and bodies what has already been accomplished in Christ.

Paul prayed for believers to have a revelation of this power. This power that raised Christ from the dead will do in the believer the same thing it did in Christ. It will not make our bodies immortal just yet, but it will melt down, undo, breakup and dissolve anything the devil has done in us. It will melt away and dissolve disease, break up bondages, undo complexes and restraints. This power will also deliver us from demonic powers and activities.

JESUS IS LORD

When Jesus was raised from the dead, He stepped from the tomb as absolute master of death in all of its phases; of hell and all of its hosts; of Satan and all of his works; of sin and all of its consequences. He was the first of a redeemed, restored, victorious humanity that would follow. He is the Firstborn from the dead; the first Man to enter the death experience and master it. Jesus is Lord!

Here is a list from Ephesians 1:19 and 20 that describes the power that is working in us as believers.

1. Exceeding greatness of His mighty power
2. Limitless scope of His power, same stupendous power
3. Incredibly immense strength
4. Great beyond measure
5. More than sufficient greatness of His dynamic power
6. Transcendent greatness - infinite might
7. Gigantic power
8. Extraordinary power, enormous over mastering supremacy
9. Surpassing greatness
10. Resistless might
11. Incredible outbursting power
12. Vast resources of his power
13. Overwhelmingly great
14. Unlimited power
15. Immeasurable, super abounding,

16. This power (the mighty force God employed) works with the force of the might exercised in Christ

17. Erupting greatness of His power

18. Excellence of the majesty of His power

The same power that is in the resurrection is in the message of the Gospel. Satan is just as defeated by the message as he is the resurrection event. The Gospel of Christ is the power of God.

REVELATION...CALCULATION

Calculate, if you can, the gigantic power behind all this. Sons, quickened into life and consciousness. We say that we believe. Yes, but what a miracle that is! It means that there is a bridge which joins time with eternity, a road which leads from earth to heaven, and the feet of believers have been set on it...Christ is in countless ways the reversal of human expectations, and in no way more startlingly than by the Resurrection. If there was one thing that all men had...to acknowledge, it was the fact that at the end of life comes death. Christ lived and died. Death had his usual triumph. But it was a short-lived mastery. "Death's pale-flag" was hoisted for a day and for a second day, and on the third day it was hauled down. And the Lamb of God, flying His own flag, was raised from the dead and entered into His glory. It was the beginning of the resumption of the original glory, which He had with the Father before the world was, but that glory was touched now with an added quality. The victory had been won within the terms of human life. The Risen Christ is victorious Mankind. In what we call the Ascension, which follows hard upon the triumph over death, the Son of God finally resumes the attributes of Godhead, but He is still Son of Man, Ambassador of Humanity, High Priest of Earth. He has taken our nature, not for one human generation only, but so as never more to lay it off, and thus it is that in Him man is now lifted to the divine level, where God is. Ephesians 1:19, 20 (Carpenter)

[1] *Wuest's Word Studies in the Greek t. Wuest, Kenneth S. (Eerdmans: Grand Rapids, MI), vol. 1, p. 54.*

[2.] *Ibid: p. 54*

[3] *Manhattan Project. Stephane Groueff. (Little, Brown and Co. Boston), 1967, pp. 355, 356.*

[4] *Ibid: p. 355, 356.*

[5.] *Strong's Concordance, G3089*

God has put us in a place where He expects us to have His latest revelation, the revelation of that marvelous fact of "Christ in [us]" (Col. 1:27) and what this really means. We can understand Christ fully only as we are filled and overflowing with the Spirit of God. Our only safeguard from dropping back into our natural minds, from which we can never get anything, is to be filled and filled again with the Spirit of God, and to be taken on to new visions and revelations.

Smith Wigglesworth

10

First Class Righteousness

The Holy Spirit never brings condemnation.
He always reveals the blood of Christ. He is
the lifting power of the church....There's not one
thing in me the blood does not cleanse. [1]
Smith Wigglesworth

Several years ago, I went deer hunting in Saskatchewan, Canada. The border official was unhappy I was there to shoot their big bucks and took extra time looking at my information on his computer. With a scowling face, he asked me if I'd ever been arrested. I said, "No," but then remembered that when

I was 17, I had been arrested, but that the charges had been dropped. The officer told me that even though the charges had been dropped, the offense was still on my record. I would need to hire a lawyer to get my record expunged, which I did when I got home. Being curious, I looked up the meaning of "expunge:" to blot out; to rub out; to efface; to obliterate, to strike out; to wipe out or destroy; to annihilate. [2] Now I have a clean record!

What God did for you in Christ is much more than dropping the charges of sin. In Christ, there is no record that you ever did anything wrong. Your situation has been dealt with in the highest court and has been expunged. Not only are you forgiven, but you are now the righteousness of God.

In the Old Testament, worshipers were accepted through the perfection of the sacrifice, not because of their perfection. In the New Testament, we are now accepted before God because Jesus became the perfect sacrifice for us.

For by one offering he hath perfected for ever
them that are sanctified. Now where remission

of these is, there is no more offering for sin.

Hebrews 10:14, 18

Notice the word "remission" in this scripture. In the Old Testament there was forgiveness of sin, but the New Testament introduces remission of sin through Jesus' blood. Remission means: "forgiveness and cancellation of sin and removal of guilt." [3] The blood of Jesus has the power to remove sin from the conscience and impart a righteousness consciousness.

RIGHTEOUSNESS REMOVES SHAME AND SIN CONSCIOUSNESS

Your mind must be renewed by a spiritual revolution.

Ephesians 4:23 (Jerusalem)

All the religions of the world come from a sin consciousness, but the blood of Jesus and the cross of Christ remove the guilt and stain of sin and produce a righteousness consciousness. **If sin consciousness could change a man, the whole world would be changed because those religions are rooted in**

sin consciousness. Entire nations are controlled by it. There are always rules or works required in order to overcome guilt. Instead of freedom, there are destructive behaviors or addictions that follow this guilt and shame. Psychiatrists teach that all self destructive behavior is rooted in shame. When anyone trusts in the grace of God, the blood of Jesus not only cleanses from sin, but removes sin consciousness.

The power of the Gospel is this: if anyone puts their faith in the fact that Jesus bore their shame on the cross, they can be made free. On the cross, God laid on Jesus, our Substitute, the shame of the world. Jesus is our Great High Priest, who can share our feelings because He was born and lived in the world as a human being. He experienced every heartache, rejection, fear and He overcame everything victoriously. Because Jesus experienced them, He can understand. Jesus now intercedes and freely gives His mercy and grace to aid and assist all who cry out to Him (Hebrews 4:14-16; 6:18,19).

The death and resurrection of Christ was the end of the old sin-cursed creation and the birth of an entirely new creation. The same power that was released in the events of the death, burial, and resurrection is in the message of the Gospel.

For I am not ashamed of the gospel of Christ: for it is the power of God unto salvation to every one that believeth; to the Jew first, and also to the Greek. For therein is the righteousness of God revealed from faith to faith: as it is written, The just shall live by faith.
Romans 1:16, 17

Listen, the Word of Righteousness contains the same power as was released in the resurrection of Christ. This is the same Word which the Holy Spirit confirms with signs and wonders. Anyone who will acknowledge it will tap into the power of God and live a life of victory. The same Gospel that saves a person will give them power to overcome in every struggle of life.

For he hath made him to be sin for us, who knew no sin; that we might be made the righteousness of God in him.
2 Corinthians 5:21

Many people would agree that Jesus became sin for us, but they have a difficult time believing and saying that they are the righteousness of God. Righteousness is a free gift not based on your performance. You can never be more righteous than the day you confessed Jesus Christ as your Lord because He gave you His very own righteousness. You can grow in faith, in love and in the fruit of the Spirit, but you cannot grow in righteousness.

Righteousness is a state of being restored to perfect fellowship with God. You're no longer running a low grade fever of guilt because now there's no sense of sin or inferiority. You are not 50% or 75% righteous, based on your good works—you are 100% righteous. What Jesus has done in redemption is greater than anything you have done. The free gift of righteousness is a revolutionary revelation.

REIGN LIKE A KING

...They which receive abundance of grace and of the gift of righteousness shall reign in life by one, Jesus Christ.
Romans 5:17

When we travel, I like to fly first class. There are privileges such as boarding first, comfortable seats and good food on real dishes. Economy class passengers get to the same destination, but never get to enjoy what is available. In Christ, there's no such thing as economy class righteousness—only first class. Don't settle for a life of condemnation and inferiority, but come up to your blood bought first class seat that has been paid for by the blood of Jesus! Because you are in Christ, you have identical status as Christ. You reign as a king and share His position of royalty.

THE SUN HAS COME UP ON A NEW DAY

But unto you who revere and worshipfully fear
My name shall the Sun of Righteousness arise
with healing in His wings and His beams,
and you shall go forth and gambol like calves
[released] from the stall and leap for joy.
Malachi 4:2 (AMP)

Four hundred years before Jesus was born, Malachi prophesied His coming. He called Him the Sun of Righteousness in whose beams there is healing. Jesus came forgiving sins and healing the lame, too. Dad Hagin would use this song, "Just as I am without one plea, but that Thy blood was shed for me" not only for salvation, but also for healing. By faith simply receive the gift of righteousness for salvation, healing and freedom from all fear.

In righteousness shalt thou be established: thou shalt be far from oppression; for thou shalt not fear: and from terror; for it shall not come near thee.
Isaiah 54:14

Thy righteousness shall lift them up.
Psalm 89:16 (Fenton)

Many are not struggling with depression but they have a lack of understanding of righteousness. When you have a revelation of righteousness, it is impossible to be depressed.

This is all my hope and peace – Nothing but the blood of Jesus.

This is all my righteousness – Nothing but the blood of Jesus.

Oh, precious is the flow that makes me white as snow.

No other fount I know – Nothing but the blood of Jesus.

[1] *Wigglesworth, S. (2001). Ever Increasing Faith.*

[2] *www.merriam-webster.com, expunged*

[3] *www.merriam-webster.com, remission*

There are many windows through which
we can look out into the world,
searching for meaning.

Most of us, when we ponder on the meaning
of our existence, peer through but one
of these windows onto the world.

And even that one is often misted over
by the breath of our finite humanity.

We clear a tiny peephole and stare through.

No wonder we are confused by the tiny
fraction of a whole that we see.

It is, after all, like trying to comprehend the
panorama of the desert or the sea
through a rolled-up newspaper.

Jane Goodall
Through a Window

...that the God of our Lord Jesus the Messiah, the Father glory-clad, may, in bestowing the full knowledge of Himself, bestow on you the Spirit which is manifested in divine illumination and insight into the mysteries of God, and may flood with light the eyes of your understanding. So shall you know what it really is, that hope which springs up in those who hearken His invitation: so shall you know what riches are comprised in the magnificence of the inheritance which He gives you among His consecrated ones: so shall you know what is the transcendent greatness of His power displayed towards us who believe—a power measured by the impulse exerted by the might of the strength of God. This He put forth in the person of our Messiah, in raising Him from the dead, in throning Him at his own right hand in the high heavens, up above all the celestial hierarchy — Dominions, Authorities, Powers, and Lordships — above every title of sovereignty that is known by any name, not only in this present universe, but also in that which is yet to be. Thus He 'put all things, like subjects, beneath His feet.' And this Supreme One has He given, as its Head, to His church, which indeed is Messiah's Body, which is filled with the presence of Him who fills the universe, with all that is therein.

Ephesians 1:17-23 (Arthur S. Way)

11

A New Day of Boldness

The Holy Spirit brings us to the realm of the revelation of Jesus Christ, so we are not living just by rules but by revelation.

> *Where there is no vision [redemptive revelation of God], the people perish....*
> *Proverbs 29:18 (AMP)*

You could say, "Where there is no redemptive revelation of God, the people are poor, sick, depressed, and defeated. Where there is no redemptive revelation of God, the people do not know the call of God, the inheritance or the authority that belongs to them." You can be redeemed and know that you are redeemed, but if you do not have a redemptive revelation, you will not be able to walk in the victory that belongs to you.

Thank God we do not have to live that way. We can have a redemptive revelation of God by the spirit of wisdom and revelation. By having the eyes of our hearts flooded with light, we can know the hope of His calling, the riches of His glory, and the exceeding greatness of His power to us who believe.

REVELATION KNOWLEDGE

An example of revelation knowledge is found in Matthew 16.

And Simon Peter answered and said, Thou art the Christ, the Son of the living God. And Jesus answered and said unto him, Blessed art thou, Simon Barjona for flesh and blood hath not revealed it unto thee, but my Father which is in heaven. And I say unto thee, That thou art Peter, and upon this rock I will build my

church; and the gates of hell shall not prevail
against it.
Matthew 16:16-18

Jesus told Peter, "You did not learn this through your five senses, you learned it through revelation knowledge." When Simon Peter received this revelation knowledge of who Jesus is—the Christ, the Son of the Living God—Jesus turned to him and said, "I'm telling you who you are, Simon. No longer will you be tossed to and fro. I am changing your name to 'rock.'"

Revelation that comes from God changes your identity. Revelation is a very personal thing. When Peter got a revelation of who Jesus is, then Jesus told Peter who he was. When you find out who Jesus is, you cannot walk away without Jesus telling you who you are.

This revelation of who Jesus is, is essential to every believer. The foundation of the church is the revelation of Jesus, the Christ, the Son of the Living God. The gates of hell cannot prevail against the church, the revelation of Jesus. The church is still being built today on this revelation of who Jesus Christ is.

The authority of the believer in the earth is based on what Jesus has already done for us in His death, burial, and resurrection. This is the center of Paul's revelation. That is why Paul prayed in Ephesians 1 that God would give you the spirit of wisdom and revelation in the knowledge of Him.

ONCE UPON A TIME

Everyone likes a great story that begins with the phrase, "Once upon a time...." The story of Jesus is the greatest story ever told. It is not a fantasy, but a true story that has changed the world for thousands of years. The story of Jesus is told in over a thousand languages to millions of people, young and old, around the world. This redemptive revelation is still changing lives today.

One day as I was studying Hebrews 9 and 10, the word "ONCE" stood out to me so clearly. I began to see God's plan of redemption in Christ and how the wisdom and power of God very effectively ONCE paid the price for our freedom.

Neither by the blood of goats and calves, but by his own blood he entered in ONCE into the holy place, having obtained eternal redemption for us.

Hebrews 9:12

He went ONCE for all into the [Holy of] Holies...(with) His own blood, having found and secured a complete redemption (an everlasting release for us).

AMP

A GREAT BEDTIME STORY

ONCE! That's all it took. What Jesus did for us in His death and resurrection, He only had to do ONCE. ONCE He shed His blood. ONCE He paid the price for our freedom. ONCE He put away and abolished sin. ONCE He dethroned and defeated Satan. ONCE for all time. ONCE for all mankind. ONCE for the cure of every condition. ONCE for every blessing in Heaven to be ours.

Whenever you face any challenge, remember this story and tell it again — ONCE UPON A TIME!

ONCE— that's all it took. Jesus defeated Satan so badly, He only had to do it ONCE. When Satan comes against you, just bring up this story and say, "Once upon a time..." and the devil will leave. Now, we as believers can take the Word of God and tell the devil a bedtime story. Say, "Devil, ONCE upon a time Jesus defeated you for all eternity." Speak the Word of God with boldness and "rock" the devil to sleep.

> *For then must he often have suffered since the foundation of the world: but now ONCE in the end of the world hath he appeared to put away sin by the sacrifice of himself.*
> *Hebrews 9:26*

> *...But as now is, He has ONCE for all at the consummation and close of the ages appeared to put away and abolish sin by His sacrifice [of Himself].*
> *AMP*

Jesus cancelled and abolished sin ONCE for all time and for all men. Also notice Hebrews 9:28,

Hebrews 10:10 and Hebrews 10:14. The Holy Spirit continues to emphasize the word ONCE. We must know this story well. It is the story of Christmas, Easter, Pentecost, and of Heaven and earth. This story is well known by angels and demons. The story of the blood of Jesus is an established fact throughout eternity.

A NEW DAY OF BOLDNESS

The other word that stood out to me in Hebrews was the word, "boldness." The blood of Jesus has given us great boldness and confidence.

> *Having therefore brethren, boldness to enter into*
> *the holiest by the blood of Jesus.*
> *Hebrews 10:19*

> *Having therefore, brethren, freedom of speech*
> *for the entrance through the Holy Place by the*
> *blood of Jesus....*
> *Rotherham*

Let us therefore come boldly unto the throne of grace, that we may obtain mercy, and find grace to help in time of need.

Hebrews 4:16

So that we may boldly say, The Lord is my helper, and I will not fear what man shall do unto me.

Hebrews 13:6

Some translations of Hebrews 10:19 translate boldness as "freedom of speech" or "outspoken." Jesus purchased our freedom of speech with His own blood. As a believer, we must be bold or outspoken. The devil does not care what you believe if you are quiet about it. Speak out what God's Word says about the blood of Jesus. Speak out who you are and what you have in Christ.

Once upon a time Jesus purchased our freedom with His own blood. Once for all time and eternity. Once for every situation. Once for all men. Boldly speak out—Once upon a time!

The blood of Jesus has given us great boldness and confidence. Who we are and what we have in Christ ushers in a new day of boldness in our lives. Instead of being a victim of our experiences, our experiences are a victim of us. Remember these two words, "once" and "bold."

In whom we have boldness and access with confidence by the faith of Him.
Ephesians 3:12

In whom we have our freedom of speech....
Rotherham

Now we can come fearlessly right into God's presence, assured of his glad welcome....
TLB

In order to access all that God has done for us in Christ, it will take the spirit of wisdom and revelation. What God did for us in Christ, He did once and for all time. We can approach the Father God boldly because of what Jesus did for us in His death, burial, and resurrection.

God has already done everything He is going to do about our salvation, healing, freedom and victory.

Our redemption is a finished and complete work. We have been permanently released and delivered from the power of the devil by the blood of Jesus. We need this redemptive revelation so we can walk in the fullness of all that God has called us to in His kingdom.

If we are to access the call of God, the inheritance that is ours in Christ, and the authority of the believer, we must have a redemptive revelation of God. Jesus Christ, Himself, gave the Apostle Paul this redemptive revelation.

For I neither received it of man, neither was I taught it, but by the revelation of Jesus Christ.
Galatians 1:12

Paul knew that this redemptive revelation was the key for believers. Inspired by the Holy Spirit, Paul wrote the prayer in Ephesians 1 so that any believer could experience this revolutionary revelation.

That the God of our Lord Jesus Christ, the Father of glory, may give unto you the spirit of wisdom and revelation in the knowledge of him: The eyes of your understanding being

enlightened; that ye may know what is the hope
of his calling, and what the riches of the glory
of his inheritance in the saints, And what is the
exceeding greatness of his power to us-ward who
believe, according to the working of his mighty
power, Which he wrought in Christ when he
raised him from the dead and set him at his
own right hand in the heavenly places, Far
above all principality, and power, and might,
and dominion, and every name that is named,
not only in this world, but also in that which is
to come: And hath put all things under his feet,
and gave him to be the head over all things to
the church, Which is his body, the fullness of
him that filleth all in all.
Ephesians 1:17-23

We can boldly ask the Father God for the spirit of
wisdom and revelation. Jesus dethroned and defeated
the devil. Regardless of who we may have been or
what we may have done in the past, the blood of Jesus
has made us a new creation in Christ. We can be
bold and confident in the presence of God because
Jesus paid the price for our freedom. Once you get a

revelation of your redemption, the only way the devil can defeat you is to deceive you.

A FINISHED WORK

I remember when our troops first went to war with Iraq after 9-11. With today's technology, we could see the ground our troops had taken within minutes. I remember when newscasters reported that American troops had secured control of the Baghdad Airport. This was very strategic. The U.S. controlled the city when they captured the airport because now they controlled who or what flew in or out of the city.

Simultaneously, however, Iraqi networks aired video footage that Sadaam Hussein was still in control. They aired false reports that U.S. troops had been defeated trying to take control of the airport.

We could see with our own eyes U.S. troops definitely had control of the airport. The Iraqi networks were airing propaganda. Sadaam Hussein had been overthrown, but he was still sending out false reports that he was in control. In reality, he had fled the city and was hiding in a spider hole! He was a former tyrant master trying to deceive people that he was still in control. The new government had to take control over the communication towers that were airing propaganda and influencing peoples' lives.

Our redemption is a complete and finished work. However, the devil likes to air his propaganda and make us think that he is still in control of our lives. Isaiah tells us that the devil may have ruled over us at one time in our lives, but because of our redemption in Christ, he no longer has control of our lives.

> *Lord, You will ordain peace (God's favor and blessings, both temporal and spiritual) for us, for You have also wrought in us and for us all our works. O Lord, our God, other masters besides You have ruled over us, but we will acknowledge and mention Your name only. They [the former tyrant masters] are dead, they shall not live and reappear; they are powerless ghosts, they shall not rise and come back. Therefore You have visited and made an end of them and caused every memory of them [every trace of their supremacy] to perish.*
>
> *Isaiah 26:12-14 (AMP)*

When we receive the spirit of wisdom and revelation, our lives will change—no more defeat. We will overcome any barriers in our lives by the redemptive revelation of who we are in Christ. We can have a revolutionary revelation and walk in the light of what God has done for us in Christ. The tyrant masters that once ruled in our lives will rule no more.

> *Knowing this, that our old man is crucified with him, that the body of sin might be destroyed, that henceforth we should not serve sin.*
>
> *Romans 6:6*
>
> *...our former evil identities have been executed, so to speak. Our old rebel selves were exterminated and that leaves us no further role to perform as offenders. We were linked with the Divine Representative in death.*
>
> *Richert*
>
> *Let us never forget that our old selves died with him on the cross that the tyranny of sin over us might be broken.*
>
> *Phillips*

For sin shall not have dominion over you: for ye are not under the law, but under grace.

Romans 6:14

Sin shall not be tyrant over you....

Wood

Sin will not be able to play the master over you any longer....

Knox

This is covered more in depth in my book *The Power of Identification With Christ*.

I pray for you constantly, asking God, the glorious Father of our Lord Jesus Christ, to give you wisdom to see clearly and really understand who Christ is and all that he has done for you. I pray that your hearts will be flooded with light so that you can see something of the future he has called you to share. I want you to realize that God has been made rich because we who are Christ's have been given to him! I pray that you will begin to understand how incredibly great his power is to help those who believe him. It is that same mighty power that raised Christ from the dead and seated him in the place of honor at God's right hand in heaven, far, far above any other king or ruler or dictator or leader. Yes, his honor is far more glorious than that of anyone else either in this world or in the world to come. And God has put all things under his feet and made him the supreme Head of the church—which is his body, filled with himself, the Author and Giver of everything everywhere.

Ephesians 1 :17-23 (TLB)

12

Revelation Fuels Dedication

In 1961, Dad Hagin ministered at my dad's church for the first time. I was just an eight year old pastor's kid and did not really pay attention to what he said. Over the years, time and time again, Dad Hagin would open his Bible to Paul's prayer in Ephesians 1 and say, "This is not a prayer for sinners or for the lost; Paul is praying for Spirit-filled believers. This is a prayer that all believers should pray!"

After teaching on this prayer, Dad Hagin stressed, "If you are not happy with your life, if you want life to be different for you, then pray this prayer for at least six months. Don't pray it one week and then skip a week. Pray this prayer at least once a day, every single day for six months. Pray it over and over again. Just stick with it until something happens. If you do that, life will be different for you. The first thing that will happen is that the Bible will become a different book to you."

WORN-OUT "RE-DEDICATOR"

At seventeen, I was a teenage boy with an afro hairdo, platform shoes, and bell bottom blue jeans. I remember sitting on the back row of the church throwing spit wads into women's hairdos, carving designs in the pew with my pocket knife, and using the church songbook to make up funny lyrics with my friends. I had actually been saved and filled with the Holy Ghost for a long time, but I knew on the inside that I was not where I was supposed to be in my walk with God. I had trouble with the world, the flesh, and the devil during the week.

I was the church's "special project." Whenever our church had revival meetings, everyone prayed for me. When I came forward for prayer, they knew it was revival time. We had a lot of revival in those days because ever time an evangelist came to my dad's church, I dedicated and re-dedicated my life to the Lord until my "re-dedicator" wore out!

Raised in a Pentecostal church, we constantly heard, "You need to be more dedicated. You don't pray enough, you don't give enough, you don't come to church enough, you don't witness enough. You just don't do anything enough. You need to be more dedicated! Something is wrong with your dedicator."

Somehow it seemed like we just needed to be a little bit more dedicated so our lives would work better. Over and over again, I went forward to pray for more dedication until my "re-dedicator" seemed to develop some technical difficulties. My dedicator kicked in on Sunday, kicked out again by Monday, and didn't start working again until the next Saturday night!

Whenever I heard that Dad Hagin was coming for three weeks of meetings, I polished up my "re-dedicator." I always made sure that I repented before he came because I knew he was a prophet. God might use him in the word of knowledge and tell everyone what I had done the night before.

Before the service began, I walked into the foyer and prayed, "Oh, God, I ask you to forgive me of all my sins. If You forgive me and forget my sins, then

You can't tell Dad Hagin and he can't tell everybody else. Besides, if he tells my daddy, my daddy is going to kill me, and Lord, I won't be of any use to You dead."

One Sunday morning as I sat on the back row not paying attention to the service, this big preacher walked in the church door. Brother F. E. Ward was another prophet—a big heavyset man who loved God, prayed a lot, and usually showed up at our church with no warning. My dad saw him and said, "Brother Ward, why don't you come on up here and say whatever you feel like the Lord wants you to say to our congregation."

Brother Ward walked up on the platform and made a few comments. Then he pointed all the way to the back of the church and said, "I want the pastor's son to come up here to the front because I have a word from God for him."

I was just a teenager sitting on the back row with a worn-out dedicator. I had just been sinning on Saturday night, and I forgot to repent in the foyer. I didn't know Brother Ward was coming. I just about passed out when my friend poked me in the side and laughed as he whispered, "You're a dead duck now!"

I got up and started walking to the front of the church. All the way down the aisle, I prayed fervently trying not to move my lips: "Lord, I'm asking You right now to please forgive me of my sins. You said You would forgive me and You said You would forget my sins. If You forget my sins, then You can't tell Brother Ward. So, if You haven't already told him, Lord, please don't tell him right now!"

By the time I reached the front of the church, I fully expected a giant flyswatter to come out of Heaven and squash me on the carpet. Then God would speak, "Let this be an example to the rest of you who choose to live this way! Put twelve stones on that spot, and tell your kids about it!"

I was expecting bad news, but when this prophet of God began to prophesy over me, he spoke to me about the goodness of God and the plan of God for my life. The love of God hit me and just melted me down. I began to cry like a baby right there in front of everybody. All I could think was, "God is so good! He's so good!"

I received a revelation of the love of God. The Bible says the goodness of God leads men to repentance (Romans 2:4). My dedicator started working better after I got a revelation of God's love and goodness toward me and a glimpse of His plan and purpose for my life.

Now I like to say this humorously because they say if you play country music backwards, then you get your house back, your wife back, your dog back, and your job back. After the revelation of the love of God hit me, I thought I should write a country western song called, "Jesus Loved the Hell Out of Me."

I don't mean to be crude or irreverent—let me explain. I went to school, and the teachers tried to educate the "hell" out of me. At seventeen I was put in jail, and they tried to rehabilitate the "hell" out of me. I went to church, and preachers tried to preach the "hell" out of me. I went home and my daddy would try to "beat" the "hell" out of me. I went to Jesus and He just loved the "hell" right out of me.

In other words, a revelation of the love of God took all that rebellion out of me. Instead of just struggling for more and more dedication, I had a breakthrough in my understanding, and a breakthrough in revelation!

REVELATION FUELS DEDICATION

After the revelation of God's love hit me like a lightning bolt, I was determined to receive more revelation knowledge and spiritual understanding of God and His amazing love. I began to pray the Ephesians 1 prayer as Dad Hagin had instructed us to do so many times. This prayer is not for more dedication, but for more revelation. Dedication is essential and important in our walk with God, but a greater measure of our dedication and consecration to God flows out of greater revelation. The more revelation we receive of God's goodness toward us, the deeper our level of consecration or dedication will be.

If Paul thought dedication was the number one need of a believer, his prayer could have sounded like a good old Pentecostal prayer:

Father God, I'm just praying right now, Lord, that You help those believers become more dedicated. Help them be more dedicated, Lord. They need more dedication, so just give it to them. Why don't they pray more, witness more, give more, praise more? Lord,

> *why aren't they more dedicated. Somehow,*
> *some way, Lord, help them be more dedicated.*

As important as dedication is, dedication is actually fueled by revelation. That was certainly news to me when I was seventeen years old. I had been raised in church all my life, but I thought my problem was my worn out dedicator. Really, all I needed the entire time was more revelation of my identity in Christ.

Now, I am not making light of dedication to the Lord. Paul, however, did not say that we need more dedication in the Ephesians 1 prayer; he said that we need more revelation. When you receive revelation from God, your dedicator will inevitably crank up a notch. You will say, "I have to follow the plan of God—I have been given revelation!"

I still wore platform shoes and bell-bottom blue jeans. I still had a big afro hairdo, but I prayed the Ephesians 1 prayer over and over again, never losing sight of Dad Hagin's instructions: "Pray it until something happens." I knew I had to stick with it. If I prayed the prayer one week and then skipped three weeks, it wasn't going to work. So, I prayed it without fail, morning, noon, and night, day after day, week after week.

> *Father God, here's what I want from You. I want You to give unto me the spirit of wisdom and revelation in the knowledge of God so that the eyes of my understanding would be enlightened. I want to know the call of God on my life, the inheritance that belongs to me, and the authority I have as a believer. I thank You, Father, for helping me to see more clearly. My greatest need is the spirit of wisdom and revelation. I thank you for opening my eyes.*

Most people never progress beyond their initial revelation of God.

Dr. Lester Sumrall

13

Growing a Crop of Revelation Knowledge

Years ago my family and I moved into a "new-to-us" home. To change the landscaping, we had to bring in a lot of dirt. In Louisiana, it rains so much that if you don't have grass growing, the rain will wash away all of your dirt. I went to see how much it would cost for that grass you lay out in squares and thought, "I spent all my money on the house. I can't afford any grass squares."

So, I went down to the store and bought a little bag of centipede grass. That bag of centipede grass cost me forty dollars. I thought there must have been a misprint on that little bag of seeds.

I got the ground ready and got out those little, tiny seeds and put them in the dirt just right. The precious seeds were planted in the ground, but the instructions said, "You must water the seeds everyday." So, everyday, morning and evening, I was out there watering with a water hose because I didn't want to buy a sprinkler.

I did not miss a day watering that seed. One night I went to bed and forgot to water the seed. I woke up around midnight, got out of bed, and went outside to water those seeds. One week, two weeks, three weeks, four weeks—everyday water, water, water. After four weeks, nothing had happened.

WATER, WATER, WATER

I went back and read the instructions: "Don't expect quick results. Don't expect anything the first four weeks. The first thing you will notice is not centipede grass, but weeds will start to grow. After eight weeks, little, tiny centipede grass will start to sprout, but you may need a magnifying glass to see it."

Then, I read some more and it said, "Be patient." Now that is not one of my greatest characteristics, being patient, but I am working on it. I thought, "I want to choke somebody." So, four more weeks— water, water, water, water—slow, soaking water in the morning and in the evening. Water, water, water!

After eight weeks, I got a magnifying glass and got on my hands and knees looking for some grass in the dirt. Finally, I saw little bitty centipede grass. After another three months went by, you could finally see the grass while standing up.

Today, the whole yard is covered with beautiful centipede grass. The planting process was important, but the instructions on the watering process were actually more specific and clear than the instructions for planting. The repetition and the watering process were essential for that seed to grow.

REPETITION—THE WATERING PROCESS

Increase comes from the spirit of wisdom and revelation. Increase in faith, increase in fruitfulness, and increase in blessing come from increase in revelation. However, the spirit of wisdom will not operate without repetition. Revelation comes by repetition.

> *I have planted, Apollos watered; but God gave*
> *the increase.*
> *1 Corinthians 3:6*

We know that Paul and Apollos preached and taught the same Gospel. Paul said, "I planted and Apollos watered." The planting would be the first time you heard the Word and received the seed of the Word. Apollos watered—he taught the same thing that Paul did over and over again. Repetition. No matter how good the seed is, no matter how good the ground is, if it is not watered properly, there will be no increase.

Sometimes people do not receive increase because they reject the watering process of the Word. Repetition is the watering process. They have good seed and they have good ground. The Word of God is planted and working in them, but they reject the watering process—the repetition of the Word.

People reject the watering process because they think, "I already know that so I'm not going to pay attention. I'm not going to listen." Even though they sit in church, they don't listen and they don't pay attention. They reject the watering process.

You can tell when people reject the watering process because there is no increase. The Word of God is designed for increase—thirty, sixty, and a hundred fold! Increase comes from the spirit of wisdom and revelation in operation. Where the Word is planted and watered appropriately, there is supernatural increase.

REPETITION BRINGS UNDERSTANDING

And having put on the new man, which is renewed in knowledge after the image of him that created him.
Colossians 3:10

Repetition is so important when it comes to revelation. Have you ever thought about the Gospel according to Matthew, the Gospel according to

Mark, the Gospel according to Luke, and the Gospel according to John? Why is that necessary? Why couldn't we just have one Gospel and one person write it? Why did God have four different guys write the Gospel? I believe it is because repetition is important, but also because each person brought out a little different perspective or viewpoint of what happened. Sometimes people can see it from Matthew but can't see it from Mark. Maybe they can't see it from Luke but they can see it from Mark. They may not see it from Luke, but they can see it from John.

In other words, God said, "I'm gonna hit you with four different ways. Surely, Matthew, Mark, Luke, or John is going to help you." Repetition. Just think about how much repetition there is in the four Gospels. I believe the Gospels are divinely inspired and designed by God because understanding is necessary. Sometimes to understand, things have to be repeated over and over again.

REPETITION AND THE SPIRIT OF WISDOM

So then faith cometh by hearing, and hearing
by the word of God.
Romans 10:17

Never underestimate the importance of repetition when it comes to the spirit of wisdom and revelation. Did you ever wonder why Romans 10:17 says that faith comes by hearing and hearing? Because it doesn't always come when you just hear the Word once—it comes by hearing and hearing and hearing and hearing. When you are hearing and hearing and hearing the Word of God, faith comes. I like to say, "When faith cometh, you knoweth."

When revelation comes, it is different from just having an interesting thought. When faith cometh, then you know faith cometh. Faith cometh by hearing and hearing by the Word of God. Revelation comes from repetition of the Word of God.

Revelation requires repetition—over and over again. Think about Paul's letters and how much repetition is in those letters—almost identical repetition.

God chose to include all of Paul's letters in Scripture because if you don't get it from Ephesians, you can get it from Galatians, Colossians, or Corinthians.

Just in the repetition department, Paul uses the two words "in Christ," "in Him," and "in Whom" over 130 times in his letters. Of those, there are about 35 very significant scriptures on redemption that need to be studied closely. One way to study Paul's letters and the New Testament is to underline or circle every time you see those words "in Christ," "in Him," or "in Whom" and see how often you see the repetition.

Repetition, the watering process, is necessary for there to be revelation. The watering process of the Word means that many times we are hearing the same thing over and over again. Someone might say, "You know, I'm just not getting it. What do I need?" Water, water, water, water, water, water—over and over again. Suddenly, increase!

The spirit of wisdom comes by repetition. That's why Dad Hagin said to pray the prayer in Ephesians 1 everyday for six months. Everyday, pray, pray, pray— water, water, water. If you stick with it, the watering process will bring increase in the spirit of wisdom and revelation.

Revelation comes by repetition—you might need to read this chapter again—water, water, water!

[For I always pray to] the God of our Lord Jesus Christ, the Father of glory, that He may grant you a spirit of wisdom and revelation [of insight into mysteries and secrets] in the [deep and intimate] knowledge of Him, By having the eyes of your heart flooded with light, so that you can know and understand the hope to which He has called you, and how rich is His glorious inheritance in the saints (His set-apart ones), And [so that you can know and understand] what is the immeasurable and unlimited and surpassing greatness of His power in and for us who believe, as demonstrated in the working of His mighty strength, Which He exerted in Christ when He raised Him from the dead and seated Him at His [own] right hand in the heavenly [places], Far above all rule and authority and power and dominion and every name that is named [above every title that can be conferred], not only in this age and in this world, but also in the age and the world which are to come. And He has put all things under His feet and has appointed Him the universal and supreme Head of the church [a headship exercised throughout the church], Which is His body, the fullness of Him Who fills all in all [for in that body lives the full measure of Him Who makes everything complete, and Who fills everything everywhere with Himself].

Ephesians 1:17-23 (AMP)

14

Cry Out For Wisdom

I prayed the Ephesians 1 prayer without fail day after day after day. For a long time, it seemed like I didn't get anything for my efforts but a dry mouth. I kept praying that prayer anyway. The day came when the spirit of wisdom and revelation kicked in. One Friday night sitting with some friends of mine at my dad's church, we studied Ephesians 2:4-6.

I was raised in church, and if someone started quoting this passage, I could finish it. Something happened on this particular Friday night, though. The Ephesians 1 prayer I had been praying for the last six months kicked in.

> *But God, who is rich in mercy, for his great*
> *love wherewith he loved us, Even when we*
> *were dead in sins, hath quickened us together*
> *with Christ, (by grace ye are saved;) And hath*
> *raised us up together, and made us sit together*
> *in heavenly places in Christ Jesus.*
> *Ephesians 2:4-6*

Suddenly, the eyes of my understanding, the eyes of my heart were flooded with light. These were not just words and just regular mental, intellectual knowledge. Revelation hit me, and I saw with my spirit eyes the light of redemption, the light of the Gospel—I saw that I was made alive with the life of Christ! The same life that God gave to Christ, the very same life that raised Him up out of hell, the very same life that made Him more than a master over the devil and death and sin—God gave that same life to me. He quickened me with the same life and then raised me up together with Him. Now, I am seated with Christ in heavenly places.

SEATED FAR ABOVE WITH
THE MOST HIGH

I never smoked marijuana and I never took LSD, but that night I got higher than a kite on Ephesians 2:4-6! I saw myself sitting together with Jesus in the Presence of God the Father far above all principality, power, might, dominion, and every name that is named. Now it became perspective and revelation so real to me that God had put everything under Jesus' feet, and then he raised me up together with Him.

I had been a slow learner, but revelation finally came. When revelation came, my perspective changed. I wasn't trying to be victorious—I was victorious because of what God did for me in Christ. The spirit of wisdom and revelation changed my perspective. Instead of trying to get the victory, I realized I already had the victory in Christ!

A breakthrough in revelation enables us to see what God sees. God sees us in Christ. We look a lot better in Christ than outside of Him. We are made alive together, raised together, and seated together with Christ in heavenly places (Ephesians 2:4-6).

When you see things from God's perspective, life will be different for you.

> *...the eyes of your understanding enlightened*
> *still more and more...*
> *Ephesians 1:18 (Doddridge)*

PURSUING YOUR POSITION IN CHRIST

Once you have seen the scenery from your seat next to Jesus at the right hand of God, you won't ever want to go back to life as it used to be. Other people may listen to a sermon on their identity in Christ and say, "Praise the Lord. That was a good point," but you will be thinking, "That wasn't just a good point, that's the way I live. I am who Jesus says I am. I have what He says I have. He lives in me and I am ALWAYS triumph in Him!"

Nothing is worse than dead, dry, confused Christianity. If Christians don't have the victory, other people are not going to come to them to find victory for their own lives. Christians must have something in their spirits that is better and greater than anything the devil can throw at them.

Believers must have a deep revelation of their position in Christ. Even in the worst situations in life, you can laugh at the devil. Your mind may be going crazy with stress and pressure as you try to think about what you are going to do. You need to stop and begin to meditate on what God's Word says about who you are in Christ. You need to see things from God's perspective. God sees you seated with Christ in heavenly places.

WAITING TO INHALE

Before we continue, let me emphasize that I in no way advocate the use of illicit drugs, nor do I intend to offend anyone by using marijuana in illustrations with the Word of God. I only hope to communicate clearly the difference between intellect and revelation. This is important because revelation changes your perspective.

Years ago one of our politicians said he smoked marijuana but did not inhale. I thought, "Now here is a man smoking marijuana, but he's not inhaling. What's the purpose of that?" Imagine, there he was at a party where everybody was smoking marijuana and passing it around. He took a joint, acted like he was really having a party, sucked it in, held it in his mouth, and then passed it on to the next person. When the person next to him took the marijuana, he breathed in and inhaled. The guy who actually inhaled reacted, "Whoa." The other guy acted like he was smoking, but he didn't inhale. That's the difference between just getting the information and getting the revelation.

That's what happens every time you come to church. Some people act like they are receiving the Word of God, but they are just kind of faking it. They are saying, "That's good. Praise the Lord!" Yet somebody with the spirit of wisdom and revelation actually "inhales" because the Word of God comes alive in them. They say, "Whoa! Jesus is talking to me, right now. God is talking to me right now. I was made alive together with Christ. I was raised up together with Him. I'm seated together with Him right now in heavenly places. I'm not trying to win, I've already won! The victory is on the inside of me!"

This is the reason why many times the faith message gets a "bum rap." People kind of learn to say the right thing, but they don't have any revelation. Many times we are very familiar with what God's

Word says about us, but we need to actually "inhale."

Back in the 1960's, a friend of mine that had been hanging out with druggies got born again and filled with the Holy Ghost after someone gave him a Bible. At first, he liked the India paper so much that he used it for marijuana cigarettes. He said, "I smoked Matthew. I smoked Mark. I smoked Luke, but I couldn't make it through John. When I hit John 3:16, I read that and got born again!"

You need to take the Word of God and say, "All right, God. Give me a spirit of wisdom and revelation." Take the Word, breathe it in and say, "I am who God says I am. I have what God says I can have. I can do what God says I can do!"

The spirit of wisdom and revelation just changes your whole perspective. You see everything differently. You see yourself, and your future differently. You see the call of God, the inheritance that is yours. You see the authority and the power you have—the same power that raised Christ from the dead. You have a new perspective—seated far above with Christ in heavenly places.

CRY OUT FOR WISDOM

In Mark 10, the blind beggar Bartimaeus, heard that Jesus, the healer, was coming his way and he made a decision that day that changed everything. Bartimaeus began to cry out for Jesus to come to him. I can just imagine his desperate voice getting louder and more determined the more people around told him to shut up and do not disturb Jesus. I can just imagine Jesus turning his direction with a big smile. Jesus heard expectation and faith in that cry. Bartimaeus had no sight, but he had a VOICE. That day he used what he had to secure what he lacked (Lilian B. Yeomans). [1] That day light broke through. That day his entire identity changed! That day those blind eyes were opened and he saw the light of Jesus. Because of his cry of faith, he was never the same again.

> *Yea if thou criest after knowledge, and liftest up thy voice for understanding. Then shalt thou understand the fear of the Lord, and find the knowledge of God.*
> *Proverbs 2:3, 5*

When you cry out for the eyes of your heart to be opened and for a revelation of Jesus, there will be a radical change. Like Bartimaeus, don't quit crying out, but go after a revelation of Christ and who you are in Him. Let your spirit cry out for the spirit of wisdom and revelation. Stick with it until you truly see what God has done for you in Christ and you understand who you are and what you have in Him. Set your mind on the reality of your redemption. Let the Holy Spirit paint a picture in your heart of you and Jesus seated together at the right hand of God in heavenly places. Then look down and say, "Devil, you are way down there, and I'm seated far above you with Jesus. God gave me the very life of Christ Himself—the God-kind of life and victory. He gave me Heaven's joy, Heaven's love, and Heaven's life. I'm blessed right now with every spiritual blessing, and you are under my feet."

Once you get a revelation of the truth of who you are in Christ, you can celebrate the triumph of Christ in your own life. Jesus already won the battle, and now, you are seated with Him in heavenly places. The joy of the Lord will bubble up in your spirit, and soon you'll be laughing at the devil.

I don't know how big the mission is that God has given you, but I do know this: ***God wants you to laugh all the way through it, secure in your identity in Christ. See the resurrected, triumphant Christ living on the inside of you. Daily declare, "The Spirit of God is in me and on me right now. I have been born of God, and greater is He that is in me than he that is in the world. I am well able to possess the land God has given me."***

The Ephesians 1 prayer is for every believer—it's for you. Determine now to pray this prayer every day for six months whenever you have a chance. Stick with it until something happens. Stick with it until you inhale and get the revelation of being seated with Christ in heavenly places. If you will be diligent to pray this prayer, the spirit of wisdom and revelation will reveal the reality of your redemption to you. When that happens, your life will be changed forever!

---

[1] *Lillian B. Yeomans, M. (2003). Healing from Heaven. Springfield, MO: Gospel Publishing House.*

...that the God of our Lord Jesus Christ, the glorious Father, may grant you the Spirit to give wisdom and revelation which come through a growing knowledge of Him, by having the eyes of your hearts enlightened, so that you may know what the hope is to which He calls you, how glorious rich God's portion in His people is, and how surpassingly great is His power when He raised Christ from the dead, and seated Him at His right hand in heaven, far above every other government, authority, power, and dominion, yea, far above every other title that can be conferred, not only in this world but in the world to come. And so He has put all things under His feet and made Him the supreme Head of the church, which is His body, that is being filled by Him who fills everything everywhere.

Ephesians 1:17-23 (Williams)

15

The Holy Spirit: Your Tour Guide into All Truth

Howbeit when he, the Spirit of truth, is come, he will guide you into all truth: for he shall not speak of himself; but whatsoever he shall hear, that shall he speak: and he will shew you things to come. He shall glorify me: for he shall receive of mine, and shall shew it unto you. All things that the Father hath are mine: therefore said I, that he shall take of mine, and shall shew it unto you.

John 16:13-15

> *And I will pray the Father, and he shall give you another Comforter, that he may abide with you for ever; Even the Spirit of truth; whom the world cannot receive, because it seeth him not, neither knoweth him: but ye know him; for he dwelleth with you, and shall be in you. But the Comforter, which is the Holy Ghost, whom the Father will send in my name, he shall teach you all things, and bring all things to your remembrance, whatsoever I have said unto you.*
> *John 14:16, 17, 26*

Jesus had spent three years with his twelve disciples instructing, correcting, and empowering them to do His works. They had seen Him function supernaturally after the power of the Holy Spirit came upon Him. In the days preceding His substitutionary work, Jesus' emphasis in teaching shifted to the Person and work of the Holy Spirit, whom He referred to as the Comforter or Helper.

Jesus told them about how He was going to leave them, He even said it would be advantageous for the disciples that the Holy Spirit come (John 16:7). Why? Because the Holy Spirit would confirm and testify about everything concerning Jesus. He would take everything Christ had said and done and translate it into their personal victory. ***"But when the Comforter is come, whom I will send unto you from the Father, even the Spirit of truth, which proceedeth from the Father, he shall testify of me," John 15:26.***

Where will the Holy Spirit come? In John 7:37, 38 Jesus said, that those who believe would experience rivers of living water flowing out of their innermost being, out of their spirit. Paul's prayers in Ephesians 1 and 3 are both asking for God to do a work of revelation and strengthening in the inner man.

BE STRONG IN THE LORD

Paul's prayer in Ephesians 3:14-21 is asking God to fill and strengthen the heart of the believer.

> *For this cause I bow my knees unto the Father of our Lord Jesus Christ, Of whom the whole family in heaven and earth is named, That he would grant you, according to the riches of his glory, to be strengthened with might by his*

Spirit in the inner man; That Christ may dwell in your hearts by faith; that ye, being rooted and grounded in love, May be able to comprehend with all saints what is the breadth, and length, and depth, and height; And to know the love of Christ, which passeth knowledge, that ye might be filled with all the fulness of God. Now unto him that is able to do exceeding abundantly above all that we ask or think, according to the power that worketh in us.

Ephesians 3:14-20

THE HOLY SPIRIT, THE GENTLEMAN

The Holy Spirit is a gentleman. He comes to do His work where He is acknowledged, recognized and invited. The moment anyone opens the door to the Holy Spirit, He magnifies Jesus. Smith Wigglesworth said with the power of the Holy Ghost, he was a thousand times bigger on the inside than on the outside! [1] He is the greater one. Paul's prayer is to be mightily strengthened according to the riches of God's glory in the inner man. The Holy Spirit is not far from the believer—He is on the inside! He supplies strength to the things in your character that may be weak. He brings a change of voice and vision to the person who has a strong inner man.

You can be strengthened as you make a withdrawal of power through the agent who is the Holy Spirit. Doddridge translation gives this rendering of verse 16: *"out of those redundant stores of goodness in his gracious heart which can never be exhausted, to be mightily strengthened by the effectual operation of his Spirit, invigorating and increasing every grace, and carrying on his work with abundant success, in the inner man...."*

We must recognize Him living within. T.L. Osborn said, "The Christian can say what no other religion can say: 'My God lives in me!'" Without the Holy Spirit, you have Jesus is only in history. With Him, Jesus is IN you! The Holy Spirit's assignment is to take all Jesus has done for us and make it a reality in us.

In Ephesians 6:10, Paul commands us to "be strong in the Lord, and in the power of his might." The Amplified Bible says, *"Be strong in the Lord [be empowered through your union with Him];*

draw your strength from Him [that strength which His boundless might provides]. The Holy Spirit abides in you to strengthen you.

RESURRECTION POWER

This strength is resurrection power, the same mighty power which raised Jesus from the dead (Ephesians 1:19, 20). Paul prayed that we would know the power outflowing Christ's resurrection. All matter is made of tremendous energy. Each atom, the smallest particle of matter, contains explosive creation power in it. Even greater is the power of the new creation. It is immeasurable!

The resurrection of Christ released enough power to not only re-create the inner man, but to destroy the old death doomed nature. Old things are passed away and everything has become new. The mighty power God used to accomplish this stupendous work was that of the Holy Spirit and the new creation shares the very same power that raised Jesus from the dead. Paul wrote in Romans 6:4 that Christ was raised from the dead by the glory of the Father and He now gives life to our mortal body (Romans 8:11). The power that God uses to strengthen the believer is glorious, resurrection power. May our inner man be strengthened with mighty power according to the riches of His glory.

THE COMFORTER

The word "Comforter" does not only mean consolation, sympathy in sorrow or distress. We are not talking about a big pillow or blanket. No, it means much more. The Greek word is "Parakletos" and William Barclay describes the Holy Spirit's work in this way:

> *The function of the Holy Spirit is to fill a man with the spirit of power and courage which would make him triumphantly to cope with life. The narrowing of the word "comforter" has resulted in the undue narrowing of the work of the Holy Spirit.* [2]

With the Holy Spirit's help, you have a Comforter, someone to stand by you, and a Counselor, one who befriends you. Jesus didn't leave us alone or as orphans, but when He sent the Holy Spirit (the Helper) He gave us a great advantage in life, in prayer and in direction.

Dr. P.C. Nelson, who wrote the Bible doctrines for the Assemblies of God and was fluent in 32 languages, had this very informative note about the work of the Holy Spirit. Parakletos, the Greek word for Holy Spirit means Advocate or Counselor, and He is called in for His excellence in three areas:

1) His exceptional knowledge

2) His expertise in protocol and procedure

3) His persuasive speaking ability [3]

The Holy Spirit is the counsel for the defense. When He is working on your case you have a tremendous advantage because He has a reputation for winning cases. He is the Advocate—the one who pleads your case. Jesus is your Advocate in Heaven, where He ever intercedes for you, while the Holy Spirit is your Advocate in the earth. He never brings condemnation, but reveals the blood of Christ.

In John 16:7 in the Amplified Bible, Jesus called Him, the Parakletos, which includes Counselor, Helper, Advocate, Intercessor, Strengthener and Standby. The Holy Spirit comes to make you strong and to help you to stand. What can we look to Him to do for us?

THE PARAKLETOS: THE ADVOCATE OR LEGAL DEFENSE

- *One who is called in to render service*
- *One who is called in to help in a situation with which a man by himself cannot cope*
- *He is the friend of the accused person. He is called in to speak in support of his character, in order to enlist the sympathy of the judge in his favor*
- *He is the counsel of the defense. He is someone who will present someone else's case to another person in a most favorable light*
- *Offers comfort and consolation. He will keep a man on his feet and enable him to pass the breaking point and not to break*

THE PARAKALEIN: THE ONE WHO EXHORTS OR URGES

- *He exhorts troops who are going into battle, rallying and cheering them to fight and to accept the risk of battle*
- *Like the speech the general gives to leaders and soldiers, cheering them on*
- *He puts courage into the faint-hearted*
- *He makes a very ordinary person cope gallantly with a very perilous and dangerous situation*

It is only when we examine this word parakletos in detail that we catch something of the riches of the doctrine of the Holy Spirit. It really means someone who is called in; but it is the reason why the person is called in which gives the word its distinctive associations.

The Greeks used the word in a wide variety of ways. A parakletos might be a person called in to give witness in a law court in someone's favour; he might be an advocate called in to plead the cause of someone under a charge which would issue in serious penalty; he might be an expert called in to give advice in some difficult situation; he might be a person called in when, for example, a company of soldiers were depressed and dispirited to put new courage into their minds and hearts. Always a parakletos is someone called in to help in time of trouble or need.

The Greek word is the word parakletos which is really untranslatable. The King James Version renders it Comforter, which, although hallowed by time and usage, is not a good translation. Moffatt translates it Helper. Comforter was once a perfectly good translation. The word comes from the Latin fortis which means brave; and a comforter was someone who enabled some dispirited creature to be brave. Nowadays comfort has to do almost solely with sorrow; and a comforter is someone who sympathizes with us when we are sad. Beyond a doubt the Holy Spirit does that, but to limit his work to that function is sadly to belittle him. [4]

I like what Smith Wigglesworth said, "God has put us in a place where He expects us to have His latest revelation, the revelation of that marvelous fact of

"Christ in [us]" (Col. 1:27) and what this really means. We can understand Christ fully only as we are filled and overflowing with the Spirit of God. Our only safeguard from dropping back into our natural minds, from which we can never get anything, is to be filled and filled again with the Spirit of God, and to be taken on to new visions and revelations." Wigglesworth also said, "It is a luxury to be filled with the Spirit, and at the same time it is a divine command." [5]

Thou shalt increase my greatness, and comfort me on every side.

Psalm 71:21

I used to play football in my backyard with the neighborhood boys. It was usually the guys my age against my older brother and his friends. What we lacked in size we made up for in great desire and determination to show how tough we were. I will never forget the day I was running a long route and turned around to catch a pass. After I caught the ball, I turned to run and at that moment I came in direct contact with the window air conditioner. It knocked me down, shook me up and I lost my wind, but I remember looking up at the boys' faces looking down at me and saying these words, "I still have the ball!"

Sometimes circumstances, people or the enemy himself may knock you down. You may have people watching to see if you're giving up or maybe you wonder if you have what it takes to win in your situation. Remember, the Paraklete, the Helper, the Greater One is in you to cheer, defend and strengthen you. The comfort He brings will revive you and bring increase as you cooperate with Him.

When Paul wrote Romans 8:26 he may have had this in mind, ***"Likewise the Spirit also helpeth our infirmities: for we know not what we should pray for as we ought: but the Spirit itself maketh intercession for us with groanings which cannot be uttered."*** The Holy Spirit takes hold together with us against our weakness to pray and breathes His life, His resurrection power and great strength through you to bring forth the will of God.

David encouraged himself in the Lord; the Lord stood by Paul in a storm to tell him to be of good cheer or comfort. We are commanded to be strong in the Lord and in the power of His might.

FILLED WITH ALL OF GOD

When you are yielded to the Holy Spirit, many things take place. One thing is that you become a body wholly filled and flooded with God Himself. All of you is filled with all of God. Paul's prayer is that the church will become a Body, *"wholly filled and flooded with God Himself," Ephesians 3:19 (AMP)*.

When you are filled with the Holy Spirit, revelation takes place. He comes to strengthen your inner man and transform your vision and your voice. One way to be strengthened is to build yourself up on your most holy faith, praying in the Spirit (Jude 20). Then you may be able to grasp all the dimensions of the love of God, becoming a Body, wholly filled and flooded with God Himself. When you are filled with God is when know what He has done in Christ. That is when you can experience the exceeding greatness of His resurrection power released to every believer.

[1] *Wigglesworth, S. (2001). Ever Increasing Faith.*
[2] *Barclay, Wiliam, New Testament Words.*
[3] *Nelson, P. (29th Printing 2007). Bible Doctrines.*
[4] *Barclay, William. New Testament Words.*
[5] *Wigglesworth S. (2001). Ever Increasing Faith.*

The Holy Spirit is a genius. If you listen to Him, He will make

you look smart.

Pastor B.B. Hankins

16

The Holy Spirit: The Genius

*And I will pray the Father, and he shall give
you another Comforter, that he may abide with
you forever; Even the Spirit of truth; whom the
world cannot receive, because it seeth him not,
neither knoweth him: but ye know him; for he
dwelleth with you, and shall be in you. I will
not leave you comfortless; I will come to you.
Yet a little while, and the world seeth me no
more; but ye see me: because I live, ye shall live
also. At that day ye shall know that I am in my
Father, and ye in me, and I in you.*

John 14:16-20

THE HOLY SPIRIT IS A GENIUS

Not long ago, a pastor friend of mine was in a Holy Ghost service where the Spirit of God began to move. In this particular service, the Holy Spirit manifested in great joy. The minister walked up to my friend and asked, "Why don't you yield to the Holy Spirit?"

My friend thought, "Yield. That's an interesting concept." He pulled out his Greek lexicon from his coat pocket to look up the word. In the Greek "yield" means when a soldier presents himself to his commanding officer for orders. [1] This word yield shows us how important it is for each of us to daily acknowledge, recognize, and respond to the Holy Spirit.

My dad used to always say, "The Holy Spirit is a genius. If we listen to Him, He will make us look smart." If we ignore Him, we look normal. If we would listen and respond to the Holy Spirit, we could avoid trouble in every area of our lives because He knows everything. We must learn to yield to and not resist the Holy Spirit.

The Holy Spirit brings you into the closest fellowship with the Father God and the Lord Jesus

Christ. If we did not need a vital relationship with the Holy Spirit, Jesus would not have sent Him to live in us. Jesus emphasized a relationship with the Holy Spirit—our helper and strengthener. He is the One who puts us over in life. The Spirit of God lives in us, and He is there to help us in every area of our lives. In this relationship, the Holy Spirit will show us truth, teach us truth, and guide us into all truth.

THE HOLY SPIRIT IS
IN "SHOW" BUSINESS

Revelation is a very personal thing. The Holy Spirit's job is to show us what God has already done for us in Christ. To understand who we are in Christ is very supernatural. We all look a whole lot better in Christ than we do outside of Him.

When it comes to receiving the spirit of wisdom and revelation, the Holy Spirit is necessary and important. The Holy Spirit reveals truth not to our minds or intellect, but to our spirit. You have certain spiritual capacities that the Holy Spirit will show you because you have been born again. The Holy Spirit is in show business!

> *But when He, the Spirit of Truth (the Truth giving Spirit) comes, He will guide you into all the Truth (the whole, full Truth). For He will not speak His own message [on His own authority]; but He will tell whatever He hears [from the Father; He will give the message that has been given to Him], and He will announce and declare to you the things that are to come [that will happen in the future]. He will honor and glorify Me, because He will take of (receive, draw upon) what is Mine and will reveal (declare, disclose, transmit) it to you.*
> *John 16:13, 14 (AMP)*

Revelation does not necessarily come easily or conveniently. You have to be determined and say, "God, I'm asking You for the spirit of wisdom and revelation." You have to stick with it. I don't know what areas you may be struggling in, but I do know that God has already done in Christ whatever you need spirit, soul, body, finances, healing...whatever you need!

The Holy Spirit can reveal and transmit our

new identity to us through the spirit of wisdom and revelation. The Holy Spirit will take what Christ has done FOR us and make it a reality IN us. The devil will try to outbluff us and make us fold, quit, and give up when there is really a tremendous reward on the table. We must understand our identification with Christ and realize that we are holding the better hand. God gave us the cards, and we win! In Christ, we are not fighting FOR victory but FROM a place of victory.

The moment you get the spirit of wisdom and revelation—Boom! You can tell the devil, "You can't whip me!" The only way the devil can whip believers is for them to not live in the consciousness or the reality of who they are in the Spirit.

You cannot understand what God has done for you in Christ without the help of the Holy Spirit, without the spirit of wisdom and revelation. Pastor David Yonggi Cho said that the Holy Spirit doesn't talk to smart people. In other words, if you already think you know everything, the Holy Spirit will not reveal anything to you. If you want the Holy Spirit to help you, you will have to become like a child.

> *I thank thee, O Father, Lord of heaven and earth, because thou hast hid these things from the wise and prudent, and hast revealed them unto babes.*
>
> *Matthew 11:25*

I've been to the zoo many times, so it's not really exciting for me, but I remember when I took my granddaughter, Avery, to the zoo for the first time. Everything was new and exciting because of her. These are things Avery had never seen before, so in her child-like wonder everything was exciting, even the fish in the pond.

God wants us to become like a child when we look at His Word. Even if we have seen a certain scripture many times before, He wants us to have a child–like wonder at the new things hidden in His Word that the Holy Spirit wants to reveal to us.

God wants to reveal Himself to you, but you need to ask the Holy Spirit to show you who you are in Christ. The Holy Spirit likes to show and tell when you ask Him. He is in show business and He wants you to see the greatest show that ever happened.

A RADICAL CHANGE

James Stalker said this about the life of Paul: "Paul's letters contain the best explanation of Christianity in the world. The right way to look at them is to regard them as the continuation of Christ's own teaching. They contain the thoughts that Jesus carried away from this world unuttered." [2]

What happened in the death, burial, and resurrection of Christ changed everything so much that Jesus had to get the Apostle Paul to write letters to the church, post-resurrection, that describe who you are in Christ. What Jesus did on the cross changed everything. Jesus fulfilled the old covenant, and God made a new covenant. The whole new covenant is that God moves right on the inside of His new creation.

The Holy Spirit showed the Apostle Paul what happened in the Spirit realm in the death, burial, and resurrection of Christ. He saw the x-ray, not the photograph, and he prayed in Ephesians 1 that every believer would have this revelation.

In Galatians 2:20, Paul said, *"I was crucified with Christ, nevertheless I live, but it's not I that live."* The Message Bible says, *"I identified myself completely with him. Indeed, I have been crucified with Christ."* People who are crucified do not survive. You cannot get into Christ and stay unchanged. You can go to church and not be changed much, but if any man be in Christ—radical change happens! Old things are passed away and everything is new. God took you to the cross with Christ, but He also raised you up with Christ in His resurrection.

When God finished with you, you were made alive in Christ. He made you a whole new creation, a new kind of creature that never existed before. You are something that never existed before because Jesus did something that had never been done before.

Jesus brought God and man back together. When you get born again, you look like a man, but you are no longer just a man. Now, God lives in you. When you are walking, God is walking because God lives in you. Paul said, "It looks like me, but it's Christ—the Messiah. The Anointed One lives in me!"

Pray the prayer in Ephesians 1 and ask the Holy Spirit to show you the reality of what happened in the death, burial, and resurrection of Christ. Ask Him to show you the exceeding greatness of His power to us who believe. Ask the Holy Spirit to show you that He not only is on you, but He also lives on the inside of you. The Holy Spirit gives us the revelation of who Christ is in us and who we are in Him.

> *Even the mystery which hath been hid from ages and from generations, but now is made manifest to his saints: To whom God would make known what is the riches of the glory of this mystery among the Gentiles; which is Christ in you, the hope of glory.*
>
> *Colossians 1:26, 27*

SHOW ME THE GLORY!

God wants to reveal Himself to us. He really is waiting for us to ask Him to show us. Moses asked God in Exodus 33, "Show me Your glory." God revealed His glory, the revelation of His name, and His goodness to Moses. David also asked God in Psalm 63 to reveal His power and glory.

The glory refers to God's manifested presence. Years ago, I studied the Hebrew word for "glory" which is chabod. In the commentary I studied, it took several English words to describe what this one word chabod means in the Hebrew language. Glory means "wealth, numbers, commerce, power, wisdom, promotion, superiority, dignity, authority, nobility, splendor, valor, magnificence, extraordinary privileges and advantages." One of the meanings of chabod is loaded or heavy with every conceivable good! [3] When we finally get the revelation of our place in Christ, we can be confident of what happens next—here comes the glory—the unlimited goodness of God!

Ask the Holy Spirit for the spirit of wisdom and revelation. Ask Him to show you His glory. The Holy Spirit will reveal the reality of your redemption to you. He will reveal the overwhelming victory you have in Christ. He will reveal to you every conceivable good that God has for you. Ask Him now, "Holy Spirit, show me your glory!"

BLUEBERRIES ON YOU AND IN YOU

But the anointing which ye have received of him abideth in you....
1 John 2:27

The disciples were familiar with the anointing of the Holy Spirit. Remember Jesus' first message:

The Spirit of the Lord is upon me, because he hath anointed me to preach the Gospel to the poor; he hath sent me to heal the brokenhearted, to preach deliverance to the captives, and recovering of sight to the blind, to set at liberty them that are bruised.

Luke 4:18

The disciples carried the same anointing that was on their Master. They also healed the sick and cast out devils. That's why Jesus told his disciples, "You know the Holy Spirit. He is with you, but let me prepare you. Something is going to happen after my death and resurrection. You are going to have a different kind of relationship with the Holy Spirit. He isn't going to just come on you any longer—He is going to move in you!"

Before Jesus' redemptive work on the cross, the Holy Spirit had never been in people. He had only come upon them. Now, as new creations in Christ, through the person of the Holy Spirit, God now dwells in us, walks in us, and lives in us.

The anointing of the Holy Spirit carries everything that Jesus has done for us. Jesus said, "The Spirit of truth isn't going to only come on you; He is going to move in you. In that day, you will know by the spirit of wisdom and revelation what it means that I am in the Father, that you are in Me, and that I am in you!"

I travel often so when I order blueberry pancakes in a restaurant, I always ask this question: "Are the blueberries on the pancakes or are the blueberries in the pancakes?" I don't want just regular pancakes with a spoonful of blueberries on top from a can. I want the blueberries in the mix. I want the blueberries to be cooked in the pancakes, and then I want more blueberries on the pancakes. I tell the server, "I want you to put the blueberries in the mix and cook them in there. Then put blueberries on top of the pancakes."

That means I can't take a bite without hitting a blueberry. I don't just have a blueberry influence every once in a while on top of the pancakes. Blueberries are in the pancakes and on the pancakes. No matter what happens, I hit a blueberry every time I take a bite!

While Jesus was on the earth, He told His disciples, "I have some surprises for you, boys. If you think what I am doing right now is good, wait until you see what happens after the resurrection. When I go away, it will be better for you because the Spirit of God that you feel on you right now, is going to move right in you. I am going to give you the same Spirit of God that's in me!"

Jesus told the disciples in John 14, you are not just going to have blueberries on you, you are going to have blueberries in you. The Holy Spirit is going to move on the inside of you and help you and show you what happened in my death, burial, and resurrection.

At that day ye shall know that I am in my Father, and ye in me, and I in you.
John 14:20

As a born again believer, you have the Holy Spirit, the Spirit of God, living on the inside of you. When the devil brings persecution or trouble to you, God says, "Life can't take a bite out of you without hitting Me." When the devil hits you, say, "Devil, what does it feel like to hit a blueberry? I've got the Spirit of God living in me. Jesus lives in me. The same Spirit that raised Christ from the dead lives in me." If a mosquito bit you, it would fly off singing, "There's power in the blood!" You have the life of God on the inside of you.

The Holy Spirit is the head of God's revelation department. As I said earlier, revelation is a very personal thing. The Holy Spirit reveals to us what God has already done for us in Christ. In God's economy, He has already done everything He is ever going to do about your redemption, your healing, your victory, and your prosperity. This is the absolute fact and the spiritual reality that you can only grasp through the help of the Holy Spirit by the spirit of wisdom and revelation.

NATURAL VS. SPIRIT

But as it is written, Eye hath not seen, nor ear heard, neither have entered into the heart of man, the things which God hath prepared for them that love him. But God hath revealed them unto us by his Spirit: for the Spirit searcheth all things, yea, the deep things of God. For what man knoweth the things of a man, save the spirit of man which is in him? even so the things of God knoweth no man, but the Spirit of God. Now we have received, not the spirit of the world, but the spirit which is of God; that we might know the things that are freely given to us of God. Which things also we speak, not in the words which man's wisdom teacheth, but which the Holy Ghost teacheth; comparing spiritual things with spiritual. But the natural man receiveth not the things of the

Spirit of God: for they are foolishness unto him: neither can he know them, because they are spiritually discerned.

1 Corinthians 2:9-14

In verses 12 and 13, Paul describes one of the primary roles of the Holy Spirit, who is the spirit of wisdom and revelation, in our lives. Verse 14 tells us that the biggest job we have as believers is to take the step from the natural realm into the realm of the Spirit. Paul makes it very clear that the things of God cannot be discovered intellectually. We must have the spirit of wisdom and revelation to understand the things of God.

In 1 Corinthians 12 and 14, Paul instructs us to desire spiritual gifts. If there are spiritual gifts, then it will take the spirit of wisdom to access them. Remember, the natural man does not receive the things of the Spirit.

NINE GIFTS OF THE SPIRIT

Dad Hagin said that the spirit of seeing and knowing would come into prominence in the last days. The spirit of seeing and knowing would be the revelation gifts listed in 1 Corinthians 12. It must be possible for us to have some seeing and knowing going on. This sounds like what Paul was praying in Ephesians 1.

> *I pray that your inner vision may be flooded*
> *with light, to enable you to see...*
> *Ephesians 1:18 (Barclay)*

The nine gifts of the Spirit include three utterance gifts—prophecy, tongues, and the interpretation of tongues. The utterance gifts all speak revelation. The three revelation gifts—word of wisdom, word of knowledge, and discerning of spirits—enable one to see the supernatural or see the unseen. The three power gifts—gifts of healings, working of miracles, and the gift of special faith—all demonstrate the revelation of the power of the Gospel. The three utterance gifts say something. The three revelation gifts show something. The three power gifts demonstrate something.

You can see that the Holy Spirit helps us in the supernatural with the power of speaking, the power of seeing, and the power of demonstration. The Holy

Spirit is our helper. The utterance gifts open the revelation gifts which then open the power gifts. As we see and say, it opens the door to the power gifts. Remember the Holy Spirit is in show business and He has a lot to show us!

[1] *Strong's Concordance, #5293*

[2] *Stalker, James. The Life of St. Paul.*

[3] *Strong's Concordance, #3519*

SECTION FOUR:
REVOLUTIONARY RELATIONSHIPS

Instead of an intellectual search, there was suddenly a very deep gut feeling that something was different...seeing that Sun...set in the background of the very deep black and velvety cosmos, seeing— rather, knowing for sure—that there was a purposefulness of flow, of energy, of time, of space in the cosmos—that it was beyond man's rational ability to understand, that suddenly there was a non-rational way of understanding that had been beyond my previous experience....

On the return trip home, gazing through 240,000 miles of space toward the stars and the planet from which I had come, I suddenly experienced the universe as intelligent, loving, harmonious.

—Edgar Mitchell
U.S. Astronaut

...that the God of our Lord Jesus Christ, father of all glory, may give you the spiritual wisdom and revelation, which are found in the clear full knowledge of Him, and illuminate your inner vision, the eyes of your heart, thereby explaining and opening to you the full nature of his calling and its aim and expectation, revealing too what an abundance of glory is implied in this "inheritance of the saints" and unfolding to your apprehension the extraordinary power which reacts from him upon all who believe. It is the enormous overmastering supremacy which the Christ showed forth, which operated in him, raising him from the dead. This power established the Christ "at his right hand" in spiritual spheres supreme in every way, untouched, unimpeded by the innumerable authorities, influences, powers, potentates of the world, having power over all other names to which authority is lent not only in this age, but in the next. God has "put all things under his feet," made him the head of all things for the Church, which thereby is constituted as the body of the Christ, that is to say, the full complete manifestation, the fullness of that one who now is fulfilling Himself everywhere and becoming all-in-all.

Ephesians 1:17-23 (Cornish)

17

Supernatural Relationships and Revelation

When I was twelve years old, I delivered GRIT newspapers in West Columbia, Texas. I had a horse named Buddy, and I would tie him up at the barber shop and deliver my papers downtown. Then Buddy and I would deliver newspapers in the neighborhoods. I think I made about seven cents a copy and wasted most of it on Cheetos, Twinkies, and Moon Pies.

One time my horse Buddy got loose and disappeared for several days. We had to put an ad in the paper to try to find him. Finally someone from another community called saying they had found Buddy. So, we went to Wild Peach to bring him home.

CROSSING A BRIDGE

While I was riding Buddy home, a strange thing happened. We came to the bridge, Buddy's hooves hit the concrete and he came right off that bridge. His eyes got real big. I kept trying to get Buddy to go across the bridge so we could get home, but as soon as his hooves hit the bridge, he turned back. I was only twelve years old and I tried to lead him across the bridge, but he just wouldn't go. We finally had to get someone else to help us get him across the bridge.

Years later, I was riding on a horse trail in Colorado. All of the horses were in one line and there was an old cowboy up front leading everyone. I rode up to the front of the line to talk to the cowboy. He had been on this trail thousands of times, so I tried to start up a conversation with him. I told him about my horse Buddy and how he wouldn't cross the bridge. I asked the cowboy, "Can you tell me why my horse wouldn't cross that bridge?" The cowboy responded, "Nobody knows."

I asked again if maybe Buddy wouldn't cross the bridge because he was a middle horse or because of something that had happened to him when he was a pony. All the other horses would cross the bridge, but for some reason, Buddy just wouldn't cross the bridge.

The cowboy responded, "Nobody knows. Some horses just won't cross a bridge."

I asked, "Have you ever had that happen to you before?" He answered, "Yep."

I asked him, "What did you do?"

He said, "What we do, is we get that horse that won't cross a bridge, and we tie it to an old horse that has crossed alot of bridges. The old horse helps the other horse cross the bridge. Then once the other horse sees that crossing a bridge ain't that bad, then he's always willing to cross a bridge."

In the body of Christ, the Lord will bring supernatural relationships into your life; people who have crossed a bridge that you have not crossed. He'll tie you together and connect you to get across that bridge they have been across. This is why supernatural relationships are so important in the body of Christ.

REVELATION THROUGH RELATIONSHIPS

So far we have seen that the spirit of wisdom and revelation is accessed first by the Word of God and then by the Holy Spirit who lives within us. The third way that the spirit of wisdom and revelation is accessed is by supernatural relationships. This is an area where we sometimes get into trouble because we fail to honor the relationships that God brings into our lives.

Too often we think we're getting along great with Jesus, yet we can't seem to get along with anyone else. We will not be able to receive the revelation and spiritual nutrition we need without honoring our supernatural relationships. We cannot treat people any way we want to treat them and then go to the Bible and ask the Holy Spirit to help us grow in the knowledge of God's Word.

Some time ago the Lord spoke to me, "There are important things that you need to know that I will not tell you. If I told it to someone you are supposed to be in relationship with, you will have to get it from them."

That brings a whole different perspective on revelation in our lives and will revolutionize the way we honor relationships in the body of Christ. Not all revelation comes directly from God, but through right relationships in the body of Christ.

SOME ASSEMBLY REQUIRED

Not forsaking the assembling of ourselves together, as the manner of some is; but exhorting one another: and so much the more, as ye see the day approaching.
Hebrews 10:25

Have you ever bought a toy for your child that has a beautiful picture on the box, but it says "Some Assembly Required." God says that redemption, healing, and blessing belong to you. He shows you a beautiful picture, but right at the bottom it says, "Some Assembly Required." There is no other way that you are going to get the benefits of this picture without each part getting in its place. Assembly is required.

You may be a piece or a part of the body of Christ, but if you are not assembled together, you won't function right. A certain part on your car might say "Manufactured in Detroit" and then say, "Assembled in Shreveport." The parts were not made in Shreveport, but they were assembled there. You may say that you are mad at the part right next to you, but the car will not go anywhere without "some assembly." You and I will be frustrated if we are not fitting and functioning in our place because that is how the life of Jesus flows through the body—when we are in our place.

If you value Jesus, the head of the church, you have to value His body and the supernatural relationships He brings into your life. The assembly of the body of Christ is absolutely necessary: "Some Assembly is Required."

One of the key words in the book of Acts is "assembled." Constantly you see believers assembling themselves not only in the temple but also from house to house. The book of Acts shows us time and again that believers came together corporately to receive from God to overcome adversity, and to receive the plan and purpose of God so the will of God could be done. The body of Christ requires some assembly.

And when the day of Pentecost had fully come,
they were all assembled together in one place....
Acts 2:1 (AMP)

And when they had prayed, the place in
which they were assembled was shaken; and
they were all filled with the Holy Spirit, and
they continued to speak the Word of God with
freedom and boldness and courage.
Acts 4:31 (AMP)

Now in the church (assembly) at Antioch...
while they were worshipping the Lord and
fasting, the Holy Spirit said, Separate now for
Me Barnabas and Saul for the work to which
I have called them.
Acts 13:1, 2 (AMP)

Paul's life revolutionized the church and still affects the world today because he was properly assembled with other believers. Acts 11 tells us that Barnabas found Saul (Paul) and brought him to Antioch and they assembled there for a year.

> *[Barnabas] went to Tarsus to hunt for Saul.*
> *And when he had found him, he brought*
> *him back to Antioch. For a whole year they*
> *assembled together...*
>
> *Acts 11:25, 26 (AMP)*

The Apostle Paul never would have fulfilled the call of God on his life without the corporate assembly in Antioch. All of Paul's letters to the church were written after he was launched from a corporate assembly. It is possible to be a part of the body of Christ and not be "assembled." There is some assembly required for believers. Being properly assembled or coming together in a local body of believers is essential to walking in revelation and fulfilling the call of God on your life.

HONORING SUPERNATURAL RELATIONSHIPS

The Bible says that when Jesus ascended upon high, He gave gifts unto men (Ephesians 4:11). This refers to people through whom God's anointing and revelation flow to the Body of Christ to reveal Jesus. These gifts may not always be the kinds of gifts we want to receive from, but whenever Jesus is in revealed, the devil is on the run. That means we need to embrace the supernatural relationships God gives us so we can receive all the revelation He desires to impart to us in our lives!

There are many examples in the Bible about leaders and supernatural relationships. We can see the value of honoring pastors and spiritual fathers when we look at Moses and Joshua, Elijah and Elisha, and Paul and Timothy.

Now Joshua son of Nun was full of the spirit of wisdom; for Moses laid his hands upon him....
Deuteronomy 34:9

Moses could not give Joshua something he didn't have. Moses must have possessed the spirit of wisdom. I'm sure that Joshua knew the exact moment when he received the same spirit of wisdom that was on Moses.

Why did Moses have the spirit of wisdom? Moses knew God. God even said, "I have talked to

Moses face-to-face," Deuteronomy 34:10. At one point, Moses hung out with God for forty days without even eating.

Moses had that spirit of wisdom and revelation. That's how he wrote the book of Genesis. He didn't receive dictation from God. Moses saw what God saw, and he wrote down what he saw. In Exodus 33 Moses said, "Show me your glory." God showed Moses the revelation of who He is and the ways of God. All he had to do was ask, and God revealed.

Joshua knew exactly what he wanted from Moses. He said to Moses, "Just lay your hands on me. I want the same spirit of wisdom that is on you to come on me because I want to know God!"

Joshua wasn't looking for an increase in intellectual knowledge about God. He was looking for a more intimate personal experience with God through the spirit of wisdom and revelation.

Elisha knew exactly what he wanted to receive from Elijah. Elijah kept telling Elisha to go back, but Elisha made a decision to follow Elijah no matter what. Elijah finally asked Elisha what he wanted. Elisha said, "I want twice the anointing that you have."

Elijah knew God and knew there was no limit. He told Elisha, "You've asked a hard thing. If you want that, you are going to pay the price for it. But if you see me when I go up, you'll have it." Elisha received a double portion because he honored the supernatural relationship God brought into his life.

Paul reminded Timothy that he had received a supernatural impartation to fulfill the call of God on his life.

> *That is why I would remind you to stir up (rekindle the embers of, fan the flame of, and keep burning) the [gracious] gift of God, [the inner fire] that is in you by means of the laying on of my hands [with those of the elders at your ordination]. For God did not give us a spirit of timidity (of cowardice, of craven and cringing and fawning fear), but [He has given us a spirit] of power and of love and of calm and well-balanced mind and discipline and self-control.*
>
> *2 Timothy 1:6, 7 (AMP)*

> *And the special gift of ministry you received*
> *when I laid hands on you and prayed—keep*
> *that ablaze! God doesn't want us to be shy with*
> *his gifts, but bold and loving and sensible.*
> MSG

The Apostle Paul knew first hand the value of supernatural relationships. Paul was launched on three missionary journeys and into his Apostolic ministry because of a corporate seeking of the Lord.

You can see from these examples that it is essential to appropriately honor those over you in the Lord. You cannot dishonor people that God has put into your life and expect to receive from them. You must honor the people God brings into your life because they carry something that is vital to you—they carry revelation. You will have to humble yourself to learn and receive these important things. God will talk to you through them and while they are talking to you, the Holy Ghost will say, "Let me tell you something else about that."

Jesus is so faithful in the body of Christ that if you are not getting it one way, He's faithful to send the Word to you in a way that you can understand

and receive it to help you fulfill the will of God for your life. Through supernatural relationships, God uses different people different ways because they carry different ingredients—they carry it supernaturally. God will use someone in your life to get the necessary ingredients to you. How you manage that relationship will determine how much revelation will come to you.

REVELATION AND RELATIONSHIPS

At one of my dad's spiritual son's meetings, the Holy Spirit moved and my mom and dad gave this prophecy. I read this regularly and keep it in front of me. Here's what the Holy Ghost said through my mom and dad:

> *It is important to take heed to the voice of the Lord that comes to you from those He puts in your pathway. Those of your brethren that He's placed alongside you to be one with you in spirit and in the work of the kingdom. Oh, it is important that your heart be open to the understanding of the Spirit to give you those things you haven't yet received in your heart.*

It will cause you to go further than you would have gone for the Lord Himself desires to open up the way where you can go further with greater intensity while the time is yet upon us and the way of the Lord and the day of the Lord is near. Now is the time to be the people of God walking in the Spirit of God and let God show you the way, every step of the way.

Take heed to supernatural relationships the Lord is prepared to show you a different path and a different way and to lead you and teach you in ways that you've never learned all the days of your life. He's able to cancel out those things of the past and to bring to you new life, new understanding and new revelation where you can walk before Him in a way to fulfill in a greater measure that which you would have not fulfilled as you're going now. But the Lord has a fresh path for you and a way to walk that would enlarge your capacity to bring ministry and power to this generation.

The way of the Lord is being made clearer and clearer and clearer to your understanding. He's shown you paths to walk in this year that you've never seen before. He's given you understanding and even the Word of faith has grown in your heart in a way that you can step forward for greater things in the kingdom of God. Oh, this is the day of the Lord. Time is not spent, it's not over, now is the time for the harvest and the plan of God to be carried out through and in His church. He's calling for a people who have a listening ear and a sensitive heart to what He has to say to you in this time in your life.

This charge I commit unto thee, son Timothy, according to the prophecies which went before on thee, that thou by them mightest war a good warfare.
1 Timothy 1:18

The Holy Ghost said—you receive the Word like the Lord is speaking to you. While Paul was in a corporate assembly, "the Holy Ghost said" (Acts 13:1, 2). Every breakthrough in the call of God on your life comes from a breakthrough in revelation. To go from one phase to the next phase, there has to be a breakthrough in revelation. God will send the Word to you in a way that you can receive it to help you fulfill the will of God for your life. We must honor the supernatural relationships God brings into our lives so we can receive the revelation that they carry from God.

REFERENCES

Note: Scripture quotations are King James Version, unless otherwise marked. Some scripture quotations are the author's paraphrase.

Amplified Bible. Zondervan Publishing House, Grand Rapids, Michigan, 1972. (AMP)

Barclay, William. The New Testament, A New Translation. Collins, London, England, 1968.

Barclay, William. New Testament Words. The Westminster Press, Philadelphia, Pennsylvania, 1964.

Carpenter, S.C. A Paraphrase of Ephesians. A.R. Mowbray & Co. Limited, London, England, 1956.

Concordant Literal New Testament, A Translation. Concordant Publishing Concern, 1976.

Cornish, Gerald Warre. Saint Paul from the Trenches. Spirit to Spirit Publications, Tulsa, Oklahoma, 1981.

Daniel J. Boorstin, "History's Hidden Turning Points," U.S. News & World Report, Vol. 11o, No. 15, April 22, 1991, p. 52.

Doddridge, P. *The Family Expositor: or a Paraphrase and Version of the New Testament. C & J Rivington, London England, 1828.*

Eddie L. Hyatt, *2000 Years of Charismatic Christianity (Charisma House, a part of Strang Communications Company, Lake Mary, Florida, 2002).p. 74. Publisher info, year.*

Gen. Chuck Yeager and Leo Janos, *Yeager (New York, NY: Bantam Books, 1985), p. 130.*

Gerald Parshall, *"The Momentous Mission of the Apostle Paul," U.S. News & World Report, Vol. 110, No. 15, April 22, 1991, pp. 54-55.*

Good News Bible, *The Bible in Today's English Version. American Bible Society, New York, New York, 1976. (GNB)*

Goodall, Jane. *Through a Window. Trafalgar Square; 1st ptg. edition (September 20, 1990)*

Gordon, AJ. *In Christ The Believer's Union with His Lord, Baker Book House Company @ 1964.*

Hudson, James T. *The Pauline Epistles, Their Meaning and Message. James Clarke and Co., Ltd., London, England, 1958.*

John Antczak, *"Experimental NASA Jet Aims for Speed Record,"Associated Press, http://aolsvc.news.aol.com/news/article.adp?id=20041115025409990001 (accessed November 15, 2004).*

John Antczak, *"Experimental NASA Jet Aims for Speed Record,"AssociatedPress, November 15, 2004, http:// aol svc.news.aol.com/ news /article.adp?id =2004111502 54 09990001 (accessed November 15, 2004).*

Johnson, Ben Campbell. *The Heart of Paul, A Rational Paraphrase of the New Testament.* Word Books, Waco, Texas, 1976.

Jordan, Clarence. *The Cotton Patch Version of Paul's Epistles.* Association Press, New York, New York, 1968.

Klingensmith, Don J. *The New Testament in Everyday English.* Kaye's Inc., Fargo, North Dakota, 1974.

Knox, Ronald. *The New Testament of Our Lord and Savior Jesus Christ, A New Translation.* Sheed and Ward, New York, New York, 1953.

Laubach, Frank C. *The Inspired Letters in Clearest English.* Thomas Nelson and Sons, New York, New York, 1956.

Lillian B. Yeomans, M. (2003). *Healing from Heaven.* Springfield, MO: Gospel Publishing House.

Manhattan Project. Stephane Groueff. *(Little, Brown and Co.:Boston), 1967, pp. 355, 356.*

www.Merriam-Webster.com,

Montgomery, Helen Barrett. *Centenary Translation of the New Testament.* *The American Baptist Publication Society, Philadelphia, Pennsylvania, 1924.*

NASA-Hypersonic X-43A Takes Flight, http://www.nasa.gov/missions/research/x43-main.html (accessed November 30, 2004).

Nelson, P.C. The Life of Paul. Gospel Publishing House, Springfield, Missouri, nd.

Nelson, P. (29th Printing 2007). Bible Doctrines. Springfield, MO: Gospel Publishing House.

New English Bible. Oxford University Press, Oxford, England, 1961. (NEB)

New International Version of the Holy Bible. Zondervan Bible Publishers, Grand Rapids, Michigan, 1961. (NIV)

New Webster's Dictionary and Thesaurus of the English Language. Lexicon Publications, Inc., 1993.

Noli, Fans. S. The New Testament of Our Lord and Savior Jesus Christ. Albanian Orthodox Church in America, Boston, Massachusetts, 1961.

Peterson, Eugene. The Messages//Remix, The Bible in Contempory Language. NavPress Publishing Group, Colorado Springs, Colorado, 2003. (MSG)

Phillips, J.B. The New Testament in Modern English. The Macmillan Company, New York, New York, 1958.

Raymo, Chet. Skeptics and True Believers: The Exhilarating connection between Science and Religion. VINTAGE; First Edition. 1 in number line edition (1999)

Richert, Ernest L. *Freedom Dynamics*. The Thinker, Big Bear Lake, California, 1977.

Rotherham, J.B. *The Emphasized Bible*. Kregel Publications, Grand Rapids, Michigan, 1976.

Stalker, James. *The Life of ST. Paul*. Zondervan Corporation. Grand Rapids Michigan, 1983.

Strong, James. *The New Strong Exhaustive Concordance of the Bible*,

Taylor, Ken. *The Living Bible*. Tyndale House Publishers, Wheaton, Illinois, 1971. *(TLB)*

The Bible in Basic English. University Press, Cambridge, England, 1965.

The Distilled Bible/New Testament. Paul Benjamin Publishing Company, Stone Mountain, Georgia, 1980.

The Hand of God. Edited by Michael Reagan. Templeton Foundation Press, 1999.

The Jerusalem Bible. Double Day and Company, Inc., New York, New York, 1968. *(JER)*

The Translator's New Testament. The British and Foreign Bible Society, London, England, 1977. *(TRANS)*

Vergano, Dan. 2005. *NASA's Bright Star, Hubble Turns 15*. USA TODAY.com, March 25, 2005. http:// aolsvc. news.aol.com / news /article. adp ?id =200 504 250 70609990009.

Verkuyl, Gerrit. *The Holy Bible, The New Berkeley Version in Modern English.* Zondervan Publishing House, Grand Rapids, Michigan, 1959.

Way, Arthur S. *The Letters of St. Paul to the Seven Churches and Three Friends with the Letter to the Hebrews, Sixth Edition.* Macmillian and Company, New York, New York, 1926.

Weymouth, Richard Francis. *The New Testament.* James Clark and Company, London, England, 1909. (WEY)

Wigglesworth, S. (2001). *Ever Increasing Faith.* New Kensington, PA: Whitaker House.

Williams, Charles G. *The New Testament.* Moody Press, Chicago, Illinois, 1978.

Wuest, Kenneth S. *The New Testament, An Expanded Translation.* William B. Eerdmans Publishing Company, Grand Rapids, Michigan, 1981. (Wuest)

Wuest's Word Studies in the Greek. Wuest, Kenneth S. (Eerdmans: Grand Rapids, MI), vol. 1, p. 54.

www.allthelyrics.com/lyrics/andrae_crouch/the_blood_will_never_lose_its_power-lyrics-1174629.html

Young, Arthur. *Young's Literal Translation of the Holy Bible. Revised Edition.* Baker Book House, Grand Rapids, Michigan, 1976.

About the Authors

Mark and Trina Hankins travel nationally and internationally preaching the Word of God with the power of the Holy Spirit. Their message centers on the spirit of faith, who the believer is in Christ, and the work of the Holy Spirit.

After over forty years of pastoral and traveling ministry, Mark and Trina are now ministering full-time in campmeetings, leadership conferences, and church services around the world and across the United States. Their son, Aaron, and his wife Errin Cody, are now the pastors of Christian Worship Center in Alexandria, Louisiana. Their daughter, Alicia Moran, and her husband Caleb, pastor Metro Life Church in Lafayette, Louisiana. Mark and Trina have eight grandchildren.

Mark and Trina have written several books. For more information on Mark Hankins Ministries, log on to the website, www.markhankins.org.

Acknowledgments

Special Thanks to my wife, Trina.

My son, Aaron and his wife, Errin Cody; their daughters, Avery Jane and Macy Claire, their son, Jude Aaron.

My daughter, Alicia and her husband, Caleb; their sons, Jaiden Mark, Gavin Luke, Landon James, and Dylan Paul, their daughter Hadley Marie.

My parents, Pastor B.B. and Velma Hankins, who are now in Heaven with the Lord.

My wife's parents, Rev. William and Ginger Behrman.

SPIRIT-FILLED SCRIPTURE STUDY GUIDE

A comprehensive study of scriptures in over 120 different translations on topics such as: Redemption, Faith, Finances, Prayer and many more.

THE BLOODLINE OF A CHAMPION - THE POWER OF THE BLOOD OF JESUS

The blood of Jesus is the liquid language of love that flows from the heart of God and gives us hope in all circumstances. In this book, you will clearly see what the blood has done FOR US but also what the blood has done IN US as believers.

TAKING YOUR PLACE IN CHRIST

Many Christians talk about what they are trying to be and what they are going to be. This book is about who you are NOW as believers in Christ.

PAUL'S SYSTEM OF TRUTH

Paul's System of Truth reveals man's redemption in Christ, the reality of what happened from the cross to the throne and how it is applied for victory in life through Jesus Christ.

THE SECRET POWER OF JOY

If you only knew what happens in the Spirit when you rejoice, you would rejoice everyday. Joy is one of the great secrets of faith. This book will show you the importance of the joy of the Lord in a believer's life.

11:23 – THE LANGUAGE OF FAITH

Never under-estimate the power of one voice. Over 100 inspirational, mountain-moving quotes to "stir up" the spirit of faith in you.

LET THE GOOD TIMES ROLL

This book focuses on the five key factors to heaven on earth: The Holy Spirit, Glory, Faith, Joy, and Redemption. The Holy Spirit is a genius. If you will listen to Him, He will make you look smart.

THE POWER OF IDENTIFICATION
WITH CHRIST

Learn how God identified us with Christ in His death, burial, resurrection, and seating in Heaven. The same identical life, victory, joy, and blessings that are In Christ are now in you. This is the glory and the mystery of Christianity – the power of the believer's identification with Christ.

REVOLUTIONARY REVELATION

This book provides excellent insight on how the spirit of wisdom and revelation is mandatory for believers to access their call, inheritance, and authority in Christ.

THE SPIRIT OF FAITH

The Spirit of Faith is necessary to do the will of God and fulfill your divine destiny. Believing AND speaking are necessary ingredients in the spirit of faith. If you ONLY knew what was on the other side of your mountain, you would move it!

FAITH OPENS THE DOOR TO THE SUPERNATURAL

In this book you will learn how believing and speaking opens the door to the supernatural in your life. God has given every believer a measure of overcoming faith. The spirit of faith will take the victim out of your voice and put victory in your voice. Your faith will never rise above the level of your confession. So get a grip on your lip!

DIVINE APPROVAL: UNDERSTANDING RIGHTEOUSNESS

One of the most misunderstood subjects in the Bible is righteousness. The Gospel of Christ is a revelation of the righteousness of God, and the center of the Gospel reveals the righteousness of God. Understanding you have GOD'S DIVINE APPROVAL on your life sets you free from the sense of rejection, inadequacy or inferiority.

NEVER RUN AT YOUR GIANT WITH YOUR MOUTH SHUT

The Bible story of David and Goliath gives us a picture of how faith in God is released through faith-filled words. Winning the War of words is necessary to win the fight of faith. We all face many giants in life that must be conquered before we can receive and do all that God has for us. Lift your voice!

HOW TO RECEIVE GOD'S EXTRAVAGANT GENEROSITY

Learn how to tap into God's supply and get results. When you put your trust in Him, you can—and will—flourish! Your generosity unlocks God's generosity. When you are a generous giver, God does things for you that money cannot do—reaching beyond your finances into every area of your life.

GOD'S HEALING WORD by Trina Hankins

Trina's testimony and a practical guide to receiving healing through meditating on the Word of God. This guide includes: testimonies, practical teaching, Scriptures & confessions, and a CD with Scriptures & confessions (read by Mark Hankins).

MARK HANKINS
MINISTRIES

P.O. Box 12863
Alexandria, LA 71315

www.markhankins.org